MONETARY POLICY
FOR A COMPETITIVE SOCIETY

Monetary Policy for a Competitive Society

by

LLOYD W. MINTS
The University of Chicago

First Edition

NEW YORK TORONTO LONDON
McGRAW-HILL BOOK COMPANY, INC.
1950

MONETARY POLICY FOR A COMPETITIVE SOCIETY

PREFACE

There are sharp differences of opinion on the subject of monetary policy—differences that cannot be the result of meager consideration of the subject. For more than a century economists and laymen alike have given much attention to this question. The differences seem to be the consequence, rather, of the fact that monetary action often has remote effects which are not immediately evident and the fact that there are competing advantages from different monetary policies which cannot be appraised in precise terms. For these reasons monetary policy is a subject which requires the exercise of judgment, and this being so, it can hardly be expected that differences of opinion will not arise. For the same reasons it is also nearly inevitable that monetary cranks of many descriptions should appear who have their "sure cures" for the afflictions of society. They see one thing that might possibly be accomplished by monetary measures, but they do not understand the many other effects of their proposals.

Nevertheless, the need for judgment in appraising monetary policies does not necessarily mean that a substantial consensus concerning at least the essential elements of a wise policy is impossible, or that we may not rate policies in relative terms of "better" or "worse," rather than in positive terms as "right" or "wrong." There is urgent need for such a consensus. A continued failure of the national legislature to come to some definite decision in this matter may have serious consequences. Yet, under existing conditions of a wide diversity of opinion, one can hardly expect the legislators to adopt a consistent policy. The economist must believe that his own position is the right one, and yet, if he is unable to convince his colleagues that this is so, he can say little more to a legislator, once he has presented his views, than "I am right, and they are wrong." The first duty of economists on public questions seems, therefore, to be that of attempting to achieve some substantial approach to unanimity of opinion among themselves rather than rushing to the public with urgent appeals for the adoption of policies which are strongly opposed by other, and presumably equally competent, "experts."

It is for the above reasons that this book is addressed primarily to economists. To be sure, in the light of the failure of economists to influence tariff legislation noticeably, one may question whether they can have any influence on public policy, even when they present a united front. Nevertheless, I am not convinced of the correctness of this pessimistic point of view and, if we are to devote any thought to the subject, I see no reasonable alternative to the assumption that in time a unanimously held opinion among economists may have some influence on public policy.

One frequently encounters the objection that a particular proposal concerning public policy, including the monetary program which I have defended, is politically inexpedient, and that it is pointless to give attention to such proposals. This point of view is indefensible. Among the things which economists are unable to do (is there anyone who is able?) is that of gauging the political appeal of a given program for public action. On the basis of the present situation, we may possibly formulate some more or less reliable guess with respect to the immediate future. Even here the failures are striking, but in any case the present is ephemeral, and public opinion shifts in unpredictable ways. What is inexpedient today may become expedient tomorrow, and present-day defenders of a currently unpopular proposal could very well hasten the change of opinion or even be primarily responsible for it. In the light of their inability to make reliable political forecasts, economists would do well to ignore entirely the question of expediency and restrict their proposals on public policy to those programs which they believe are inherently the most desirable. It is also to be noted that one who espouses the cause of expediency comes close to asserting that one should never be in the minority on questions of policy.

I am greatly indebted to Professor Milton Friedman, who has read the penultimate draft of the manuscript. In consequence of his many suggestions several chapters have been rewritten and others have been revised to a greater or lesser extent. I am also grateful to Professor Clarence Philbrook, who has read the manuscript carefully and whose comments have been exceedingly helpful. To my late colleague, Professor Henry C. Simons, I owe much. I have been influenced by him to an immeasurable extent, both as to the fundamental importance of monetary stability in a competitive society and as to the details of a desirable monetary system. I could easily extend the list of names of my associates from whose knowledge and wisdom I have benefited, but since there could be no clear-cut stopping place to such an extension, it had best not be attempted.

LLOYD W. MINTS

CHICAGO, ILL.
July, 1950

CONTENTS

Preface v

1. Stability and Monetary Policy 1

2. Two Nonmonetary Types of Unemployment 15

3. The Propensity to Hoard and Unemployment 29
Appendix to Chapter 3 52

4. Internal Adjustments to International Disturbances 71

5. Fixed versus Flexible Exchange Rates . . 91

6. The Guide for Monetary Action . . . 115

7. The Guide for Monetary Action (*Continued*) . 143

8. The Implementation of Monetary Policy . 175

9. The Implementation of Monetary Policy (*Continued*) 191

Index 231

Chapter 1

STABILITY AND MONETARY POLICY

I

There is a widespread belief that a competitive organization of economic life is inherently unstable. It is contended that either periodic or continuous unemployment at an intolerably high level is unavoidable in an economy of free markets. This attitude assumes to be true a point of view which is, at the least, debatable. So far as the evidence goes, the alternative conclusion—that the shortcomings of the system in the past have been due to failure to provide the necessary rules and conditions for the effective functioning of a competitive economy—is equally plausible.

In this connection we should distinguish between the general equilibrium of neoclassical theory and what may be termed monetary equilibrium. In accordance with the former, resources are allocated in such manner as to yield substantially the same rate of return on investment in all industries. This equilibrial allocation of resources will prevail, however, only if there is a fair measure of competition, if relative prices of commodities and services are reasonably flexible, and if there is substantial monetary stability. A change in tastes or in cost conditions will cause changes in relative prices and rates of return, and these in turn will give rise to shifts of resources which will continue until equality of return on investment is restored. These responses to disturbances are spontaneous, prompt, continuous; and they provide adjustments in a constantly changing economy which are in accordance with the desires of the public.

Monetary equilibrium is a quite different matter. It implies an absence of either boom or declining output and employment. There are numerous kinds of disturbances which will "push" the economy in the direction of either boom or depression; and under the conditions of monetary uncertainty that have heretofore prevailed, to such disturbances the system has provided no immediate, spontaneous responses which will quickly restore equilibrium. On the contrary, such autonomous responses as there have been have tended, for a limited period of time, to be disequilibrating in character and, therefore, to aggravate the difficulty. In the light of history the public is justified in believing either that there will be no monetary action or that such action as may be taken will be long delayed and perhaps of the wrong kind. The resulting anticipations of the public and the perverse action of the banks have been ample to accentuate an undesirable trend and, therefore, to magnify fluctuations in employment and output. This failure of the system immediately to provide corrective responses to disturbances is in sharp contrast with the spontaneous reactions that are ever occurring to re-establish and maintain general equilibrium. It is my thesis, however, that the absence of such responses is not inherent in the system, but that it results from our failure to provide conditions of monetary stability. It is the implementation of a competitive economy that is at fault, not the competitive order itself.

Our recommendations for remedial measures will depend upon our conclusions with respect to the reasons for the past shortcomings of the system. If we believe that they are inherent, we shall demand either the adoption of measures which will directly combat unemployment, whether temporary or chronic, or outright collectivism. If, on the other hand, we conclude that it is the implementation that is at fault, we shall seek to discover and provide such essential rules for the functioning of a competitive system as are now lacking.

The preponderance of current reform proposals reflects a strong feeling of doubt about the merits of free markets. This is true even among many of those who are opposed to an outright collectivist economy. Necessarily such skepticism leads to a belief that the state is directly responsible for the maintenance of employment and output. This point of view has been clearly stated by Sir William Beveridge: [1]

> It must be a function of the State in future to ensure adequate total outlay and by consequence to protect its citizens against mass unemployment, as definitely as it is now the function of the State to defend the citizens against attack from abroad and against robbery and violence at home.

Logically this attitude leads to proposals for public employment for those unemployed by private industry, for governmental support of aggregate demand in some manner. Proposals of this kind typically fail to take into account either the effect on the whole political and economic structure of the remedial measures offered or the possibility that general and indirect measures would be more effective.

II

It must be conceded, as Sir William implies, that in a competitive system it is not within the power of the individual business enterprise to provide the necessary conditions for the maintenance of stability and a high level of output. Exhortations to businessmen to pursue policies which will maintain employment are largely wasted effort. Individuals cannot do so even if they would. In a competitive economy it is the function of the state to provide the necessary rules for the satisfactory operation of the

[1] William H. Beveridge, *Full Employment in a Free Society* (American ed., W. W. Norton & Company, Inc., 1945), p. 29.

system. The responsibility of the state for maintaining employment is indirect. It is met if provision is made for such over-all requirements as flexible prices and stability of monetary conditions. It is my thesis that if such rules are provided no direct remedies for unemployment will be required.

It has been too frequently assumed that a mere minimization of governmental activities, a complete abstention by the government from "interference" with the economic affairs of the nation—a policy, that is, of pure *laissez faire*—will yield satisfactory results if such can be obtained from a competitive system. This is a wholly mistaken view. It has led to the formation of monopolistic restrictions of many kinds; but of more immediate present relevance, this attitude has been in considerable measure responsible for the development of fractional reserve banking and for the failure on the part of the government to assume explicit and adequate responsibility for monetary policy.

During the nineteenth century, adherence to the concepts of *laissez faire* led many to believe that the issuance of bank notes against fractional reserves was a "right" of anyone who desired to engage in this activity. It was further contended by many that no regulation or control of the banks was necessary, that free and competitive banking would operate to promote the welfare of the community. While these views were not unanimously held, it is clear that they, perhaps together with a lack of clear understanding of the nature of banking, were adequate to prevent rational legislation on this subject.

If a malignant despot desired to create the utmost confusion among his subjects on questions of public policy, he would surely require that any question of importance invariably be considered jointly with at least one other, unrelated, problem; and if he had a real genius as his adviser, the latter would immediately suggest that joint discussion of private lending operations and monetary policy would serve the purposes of his master very nicely.

Commercial banking presents precisely this incongruous mixture in practice, and therefore the confusion in discussions of monetary and banking policy should occasion no surprise.

Ideally all private lending operations, or any placing of funds which the possessor does not desire to use in the hands of one who will use them, would be merely a transference of money income and, consequently, of market control over a certain quantity of resources, from one person to another. Monetary policy, on the other hand, is a matter of controlling the total volume of circulating medium in accordance with some reasonable criterion. With a sensible financial structure, these two problems would have nothing in common. It would seem that an evil designer of human affairs had the remarkable prevision to arrange matters so that funds repayable on demand could be made the basis of profitable operations by the depository institutions. It is wholly fortuitous that an income can be earned from the use of such funds, but this being so has resulted in the creation of institutions which have largely taken over the control of the stock of money, an essential governmental function. To compound our difficulties, a whole theory of monetary control has been created upon the basis of commercial banks, which are at the best unnecessary and at the worst a highly aggravating influence in business fluctuations.

Bankers are an intimate part of the business community, and they are more than likely to share the expectations of their associates. Their lending will be influenced accordingly. They are creditors on short term. If business conditions are not good, the bankers are therefore in a position to curtail their lending; and this they are impelled to do, both because they fear outright losses on new loans and because of the danger of a demand for cash. To this danger they are necessarily hypersensitive, since they are debtors on both short term and demand, and their reserves are insufficient to meet all possible demands.

Furthermore, the banks are worse than mere thoroughgoing fractional reserve institutions. They operate with a most unfortunate mixture of 100 per cent and fractional reserve requirements. They may not issue notes to be used as hand-to-hand currency, which is equivalent to a right of note issue with a requirement of 100 per cent reserves; but against their deposits they are required to hold only fractional reserves. These conditions mean that any demand by the public to convert deposits into hand-to-hand currency must be met from the reserves of the banks, and the mere fact of conversion from one form of money into another therefore may require a multiple contraction of the volume of bank loans and of the stock of money. However, it should be noted that the institution of deposit insurance must surely have reduced the danger from this source to some uncertain extent. A large proportion of depositors now would have much less reason than formerly to convert deposits into legal tender if they feared that the banks were unsound; although even those whose deposits were insured might to some extent demand cash merely because they feared that their funds would be made available to them, in case of failure, only after some delay.

Prior to 1934 it was inevitable that the banks should vary their lending perversely, and that they should thereby aggravate, and possibly even initiate, periods of disturbance. It is unlikely that deposit insurance has eliminated all of this unfortunate characteristic, since it cannot have eliminated other reasons for this perversity than the withdrawals of cash which the public is likely to make when doubts about the condition of the banks prevail. There is no force within the banking system which tends at any time to adjust the volume of bank loans spontaneously to the requirements of monetary stability. To be sure, many writers, from Adam Smith to the present time, have contended that the restriction of bank loans to bona fide, short-term, commercial purposes constitutes such a factor. In fact, however, this "real-bills" doctrine is almost wholly fallacious.[2] The requirement that some relatively small amount of reserves in cash be maintained does indeed place an upper limit upon the amount of liabilities that a bank may incur, but this limit itself is unlikely to be consistent with the requirements of monetary policy; and in any case the actual volume of deposits fluctuates in greater or less degree as the fears and hopes of the borrowers and the bankers alike shift from time to time. However, the banks have now become so enmeshed in the economic structure that it would be difficult to eliminate them, and it is almost equally difficult to obtain the necessary perspective from which to secure an accurate view of their essential nature. Even more remarkable than the permission given the banks to develop is the apparent belief among many writers that they are beautifully designed to serve as instruments for the implementation of monetary policy.

However, we should not exaggerate the shortcomings of the banks. Even though, in their role as combined lenders and receivers of demand deposits, they constitute no positively desirable element in the economy, it does not follow that their operations might not be rendered substantially innocuous. For the most part the banks have probably been accentuating factors in business fluctuations rather than initiators of disturbances, and while in this way they have without much doubt been one of the major reasons for the more extreme swings in output and employment, it is nevertheless probable that under conditions of monetary stability the banks would, to a minor extent only, operate either to aggravate or to initiate changes in the level of business activity.

The international gold standard would have introduced into the monetary system a significant degree of stability had it been permitted to operate as a genuinely automatic standard. However, the operations of the banks made the

[2] For a defense of this statement see Lloyd W. Mints, *History of Banking Theory*, pp. 30–38.

quantitative relation between gold and the stock of money tenuous and uncertain. As a consequence the gold standard before 1914 was of little aid in providing monetary equilibrium. Nevertheless, conditions became much worse after the First World War. During the years from about 1880 to 1913, belief in the desirability of a central bank gradually grew in the United States, although there was difference of opinion as to precisely what a central bank could and should do and as to the extent of the power that should be given to it. During the 1920's this belief was greatly strengthened, and what were held to be the goals of central-bank action were more explicitly formulated. The most unfortunate aspect of this development was the general belief that the central bank should be given wide discretionary powers to take whatever action seemed to it wise in given circumstances. The Federal Reserve System was created and was operated (and still is) in accordance with this point of view.

The consequence of all these developments is that today we have utter confusion and uncertainty in our monetary system. We do not know when or to what extent the banks may extend or contract the stock of money; we do not know what policy the Federal Reserve System will pursue. Who would have predicted before 1929 that the Reserve System would take an almost completely passive attitude during conditions such as those that developed from 1929 to 1932? And who, at the time of the entrance of the United States into the war in 1941, would have predicted that not only throughout the war but for four years (and how many more?) following the close of the war, the Reserve System would consider its primary function to be that of stabilizing the government bond market? And who today can predict what action the Reserve System will take under any given circumstances? If we may judge from history, there is a fair prospect that the action of the System will be unfortunate at the very least. However, even though the System should take the most desirable action as of the moment, the course pursued by the System is nevertheless quite inadequate, in that it fails to adopt and announce a definite policy which the public can rely upon.

III

While there are no inherent factors in a competitive system which will initiate monetary instability, such a system is nevertheless susceptible to exogenous disturbances, particularly if a large proportion of income is saved and is invested by others than the savers. The consequence is that in the absence of a definite program for monetary stability—and especially if the monetary system exhibits the perverse elasticity which is the inevitable concomitant of uncontrolled fractional-reserve banking—fluctuations in employment will occur with a frequency and a severity that will be intolerable. Nevertheless, the critics too hastily conclude that the market cannot be an effective device for organizing economic activities—that it is the market device itself which is at fault. They ignore the fact that the required offsets to disturbances fail spontaneously to appear only because we do not provide the necessary conditions for their emergence.

One of the prime requisites for the automatic and effective functioning of a competitive system is monetary stability. A deliberately provided, definite, and known monetary policy is a unique and indispensable means of reducing to a minimum variations in the expectations of the public. It is as much an essential part of the framework of an enterprise economy as is competition or the law of contracts.

The great majority of economists have held that a stable price level is desirable, although there has been and is difference of opinion as to the proper index to be used as the indicator of stability. Although his proposed monetary system was badly misconceived, John Law saw this need. Ricardo believed stability desirable, but he saw no possibility of measuring changes in the price level or of obtaining a nearer approach to stability than would be furnished by the gold standard. In more recent years, Irving Fisher has been the strongest supporter of a policy of stabilizing the price level. However, the overwhelming preponderance of opinion has been that a stable purchasing power of money is merely *desirable;* that it should be provided, if at all, primarily as a matter of justice to debtors, creditors, and fixed-income receivers. Monetary stability, as evidenced by a stable price level, has seldom been looked upon as a necessary condition for the effective operation of a competitive system. Nevertheless, some few writers have seen the essential need for monetary stability and have proposed deliberate efforts to maintain price-level stability for this reason, rather than merely on grounds of justice. So far as my knowledge goes, the earliest writer who took this position was Erick Bollman. In 1811 he wrote as follows: [3]

> Since, however, prosperity in our state of civilization and trade depends on industry, and industry on security in its broadest sense—on security not only of person, of property, but also of calculation—it is of the utmost importance that extraordinary and general changes of prices, such as arise, not from occasional and natural variations in demand and supply, with regard to one or another commodity, but from a sudden and considerable diminution or increase of circulating medium, should be as much as possible avoided. No change should be suffered which would materially affect the debtors or creditors of former years, and consequently deter the active men of the day from contracting engagements, or exercising their means. This should be attended to; not only from principles of justice, but also from motives of convenience and policy; because such revolutions in nominal value baffle all rational calculations, impair security, destroy industry, and thus undermine the very foundation of national power and wealth.

[3] "A Letter to Alexander Baring, Esq., on the Present State of the Currency of Great Britain," *American Review of History and Politics,* II (1811), 255. Published anonymously.

J. M. Keynes asserted that rigidity of wage rates furnishes the needed factor of stability to prevent the system from plunging toward ever lower levels of output. Apparently he came to this conclusion because he based his analysis upon a tacit and seemingly unconscious assumption of the monetary chaos that has been provided in the past by fractional-reserve banking and the unpredictable and often perverse decisions of central bankers uncontrolled by legislatively established rules.[4] While his recommendations on policy did, indeed, include deliberate variations in the stock of money, he offered no precise criterion for monetary action that might serve to stabilize the expectations of the public. His failure to give due weight to this matter is the more surprising in the light of an earlier statement by him that is clear and emphatic. It runs as follows:[5]

> The Individualistic Capitalism of today, precisely because it entrusts saving to the individual investor and production to the individual employer, *presumes* a stable measuring-rod of value, and cannot be efficient—perhaps cannot survive—without one.

Henry C. Simons saw most clearly the essential character of the need for monetary stability. While he believed that stabilization of the price level is (for the present, at least) the most feasible policy for this purpose, he was much more interested in pointing out the urgent need for *some* definite and announced criterion than in this, or any other, specific indicator of stability. His work was consistently directed toward the statement of the proper rules and condi-

[4] "In fact we must have *some* factor, the value of which in terms of money is, if not fixed, at least sticky, to give us any stability of values in a monetary system." [J. M. Keynes, *The General Theory of Employment, Interest and Money* (Harcourt, Brace and Company, Inc., 1936), p. 304.] We need, not a factor stable in terms of money, but money stable in terms of goods and services in general.

[5] J. M. Keynes, *Monetary Reform* (Harcourt, Brace and Company, Inc., American ed., 1924), p. 45.

tions for the effective functioning of a competitive society, and he looked upon a rule for monetary stability as one of the most important of such conditions. He wrote this excellent summary of his position:[6]

> A democratic, free-enterprise system implies, and requires for its effective functioning and survival, a stable framework of definite rules, laid down in legislation and subject to change only gradually and with careful regard for the vested interests of participants in the economic game. It is peculiarly essential economically that there should be a minimum of uncertainty for enterprisers and investors as to monetary conditions in the future—and, politically, that the plausible expedient of setting up "authorities" instead of rules, with respect to matters of such fundamental importance, be avoided, or accepted only as a very temporary arrangement. The most important objective of a sound liberal policy, apart from the establishment of highly competitive conditions in industry and the narrow limitation of political control over relative prices, should be that of securing a monetary system governed by definite rule.

Monetary stability does not imply that there is any unique criterion of stability; but it does require that we choose from among the various possibilities some one, and only one, criterion for monetary action; and that we restrict the monetary agency rigorously to adherence to that choice. This choice (1) should provide, as nearly as possible, complete certainty concerning the nature of monetary action that will be taken under all circumstances, and (2) should be such that the monetary action required will not itself necessitate adjustments that will be difficult to make. The importance of each of these two aspects of the criterion chosen can be sharply brought out by asking ourselves which would be worse: (1) our present monetary uncertainty, or (2) an announced policy of increasing and de-

[6] Henry C. Simons, "Rules versus Authorities in Monetary Policy," *Journal of Political Economy,* XLIV (1936), 29. Reprinted in *Economic Policy for a Free Society* (1948), pp. 160–183.

creasing the stock of money in alternative years by 10 per cent. Fortunately we are not faced with any such difficult choice.

If we assume a reasonably flexible price structure, and if, for example, we adopted a policy of stabilizing an index of the price level, any decline in aggregate demand would be reflected in the index. A decline in the index would call for an increase in the stock of money by the monetary agency; but, of perhaps greater importance, declining prices would mean rising real value of the cash balances of the public.[7] Under these circumstances the public would not for long postpone an increase to former levels of their purchases of either securities or commodities. If, instead, monetary policy called for complete fixity in the stock of money, the same rise in the real value of cash balances would take place, and thus again reestablishment of a satisfactory level of aggregate demand would not long be delayed. It should be noted, however, that it might not be possible to achieve a high and stable level of output with a fixed stock of money unless a degree of price flexibility could be obtained which in practice may be unattainable.

Furthermore, quite aside from the response of the public to a change in the real value of their cash balances, the definite and known monetary policy would do much to stabilize expectations, and thus changes in aggregate demand would in the first instance be greatly reduced as compared with conditions in the past. I should expect this to be the most important factor in maintaining output and employment at a high level.

There are other reasonable criteria of monetary action that might be adopted, although I shall defend stabilization of a price-level index as the most feasible when all considerations are taken into account. This defense, together

[7] The manner in which open market operations and budget deficits and surpluses might be expected to affect aggregate demand will be examined in Chap. 9.

with some examination of other policies, will be found in Chapters 6 and 7. In any event, the problem is not that of discovering the most effective means of combatting deflation or inflation. If we had stability of expectations in regard to monetary matters and flexible individual prices—product prices, wage rates, and interest rates—we might then rely upon the spontaneous responses of the system not only to allocate the resources at the disposal of the community, but to maintain a satisfactory level of output and employment. Nevertheless, monetary stability is not a specific remedy for fluctuations in employment. The needed policies are general in nature—policies that will serve our purposes indirectly, through the promotion of the autonomous reactions that will maintain a satisfactory approach to stability in aggregate demand—and monetary policy is of this kind.

Chapter 2

TWO NONMONETARY TYPES OF UNEMPLOYMENT

I

Unemployment can be considered from three points of view. (1) There are fluctuations in employment induced by variations in the propensity to hoard cash or by inappropriate changes in the stock of money. (2) There is frictional unemployment, which is the consequence of frequent or continuous change in economic conditions, while at the same time there are factors which retard the adjustments necessary for the reestablishment of general equilibrium. (3) There is the possibility of a permanently low level of employment brought on by the success of labor monopolies in raising wage rates in virtually all occupations above the marginal productivity of the workers under conditions of full employment.

Variations in the propensity to hoard cash are caused by numerous factors, and yet the resulting fluctuations in the velocity of circulation of money will have the same effect as an inappropriate change in the volume of money. Both in this sense and in the further sense that variations in aggregate demand due to these causes are controllable by monetary measures, the first type of unemployment listed above is essentially a monetary phenomenon. The frequent recurrence of unemployment caused by these monetary factors is, therefore, one of the major reasons for desiring a policy of monetary stabilization. Unemployment of this kind will be considered in Chapter 3.

The second and third types of unemployment are non-monetary in origin, and monetary measures can be of no more than minor assistance, if at all, in dealing with them. They are therefore essentially irrelevant to the purposes of this essay, and yet some discussion of them seems necessary to make this evident. This chapter will be briefly devoted to that task.

II

In a changing economy continual reallocation of resources will be required. This fact will result in some unavoidable amount of unemployment unless men can shift from one job to another instantaneously. In practice there is likely to be present one or more of four impediments to the elimination of this frictional unemployment. These are as follows: (1) rigidity of product prices, (2) rigidity of wage rates, (3) lack of homogeneity in the labor force, and (4) labor immobility geographically. Immobility is primarily due to (*a*) lack of knowledge of opportunities for employment, (*b*) the cost to the laborer of moving from one locality to another, and (*c*) reluctance to leave the home environment. No one of these four factors by itself can create any substantial amount of unemployment, but any combination of two or more, with the exception of the combination of rigid product prices and rigid wage rates, can cause a continuing volume of unemployment, great or small.

If the labor supply of the community were homogeneous, if workers had full knowledge of all opportunities for employment, if there were no costs of transportation of workers, and if workers were willing to move with changes in conditions, employment would be maintained despite any shifting of demand and without any (substantial) change in wage rates. To be sure, diminishing returns might apply more sharply to the industries to which demand had shifted than to those in which demand had been reduced, and this fact would require some reduction in the wage level; but this change would be inconsequential in any given short period of time. If this high degree of mobility of labor does not prevail, any change in demand will require some flexibility in wage rates if unemployment is to be minimized.

Suppose the demand schedule for the final product of an industry shifts downward. If costs are to be reduced sufficiently to maintain output through the medium of a reduction of the cost of any one ingredient, that reduction will have to be relatively larger than the decrease in the price of the final product. Moreover, no reduction at all will be possible for those ingredients which are unspecialized and, therefore, much used in other industries. Raw materials are good examples. If a 10 per cent reduction in the price of the product is to be achieved by means of a reduction in the rate of pay of only one class of workers, whose wages make up 50 per cent of the variable costs, then the wage reduction may have to be close to 20 per cent. It may not have to be quite so much if, in addition to the direct cost reduction due to this decrease in wage rates, the industry finds it possible further to reduce costs by substituting these laborers for other factors the prices of which will not have been reduced. Granted flexibility in the price of the final product, it is evident that wage reductions could reduce frictional unemployment to very low levels, but that the reduction might have to be drastic in view of the fact that the prices of many other factors cannot be reduced.

The function of the reduction in wage rates might be said to be that of maintaining employment pending a retraining (if the labor force is not homogeneous) and reallocation of the labor force. The reduction, however, will be only temporary if in time the obstacles to mobility are overcome. Meanwhile the income of both the workers and the owners in the industry will be reduced; but the counterpart to this decline will be an increase in incomes in the industries to which demand has shifted, provided aggregate demand is maintained. Both the reduction of incomes in the one industry and the increase in the others, will lead to further shifts in demand, and thus the repercussions become so complicated as to make it impossible to follow them in detail.

If the shift in demand were of large proportions relative to the whole economy, and if the reduction in wage rates were not prompt, aggregate income and demand might significantly decline in the absence of an established policy of monetary stabilization. In this case frictional unemployment shades off into "mass" unemployment; and while monetary action can do nothing directly to prevent the former, it can prevent it from developing into a disastrous general decline in employment. However, a continuous succession of minor shifts in demand should cause no more than a relatively constant volume of unemployment under conditions wherein wage rates are inflexible. Changes in demand for individual products are not likely often to *initiate* the cumulative downward course of employment and output.

If the price of the final product is inflexible, the change in demand conditions will have its full effect on the volume of output and employment, with possibly minor alleviatory effects from wage flexibility, and the number of workers who will be compelled immediately to seek employment elsewhere will be relatively large. The minor effect, if present, would come from the substitution of the now cheaper labor for factors that had not gone down in cost, and not from any limitation of the decline in output.

A technological innovation will give rise to somewhat more complicated adjustments. However, it is necessary to stipulate the monetary policy that prevails as a basis for an analysis of this question. Let us assume, then, that the price level is permitted to fall with advances in technology, which will mean that wage rates will be constant, and substantially product prices also, except those of products subject to cost reductions. This assumption may require that the quantity of money be increased very gradually, even though the population should be stable and the velocity constant. If the quantity of money is increased, then total money income (but not wage rates) will also rise gradually. The increase in the quantity of money will be required by increasing capital accumulation unless the rate of interest falls sufficiently to prevent a rise in the total real earnings from investment. Actually, an innovation will tend to raise the rate of return for a short period of time, and therefore, for the purpose of analyzing the effect of innovations on frictional unemployment, we may ignore the long-run possibility that the rate of return may gradually decline. If, then, the real earnings from investment rise, a larger proportion of the income of the community will be going to investors, and if this development is not to bring on a reduction in wage rates or in the prices of products for which there has been no cost reduction, the quantity of money must be increased. To be sure, the real income of the wage earners will also be rising, since their money incomes will be constant and the prices of (some) commodities will be falling.

Let us assume an improvement in the equipment used in the production of a consumers' good. First will come the effect on the equipment-producing industries. The demand for producers' goods at a given rate of interest will rise; but since it is unlikely that the volume of savings will rise before the effect of the innovation is realized in increased output, we must assume that the rate of interest will rise sufficiently to maintain near constancy in the aggregate output of investment goods. To be sure, it is possible that the rise in the rate will bring forth a larger volume of savings and that equilibrium for the time being will be reached with both a higher rate of interest and a larger output of producers' goods. In any case, the increased amount of equipment demanded by the innovating industry will be obtained, to some extent at the very least, at the expense of other equipment that would have been produced in the absence of the innovation. If the new types of investment goods are so different from those at the expense of which they are produced that they must be produced by a different firm or industry, there will be required a reallocation of resources among the producers' goods industries. This development can be analyzed in much the same way as the change in the demand for consumers' goods.

The nature of the demand for the product of the industry introducing the innovation will have a bearing on the adjustments required. If the elasticity of demand is less than one, other industries will find the demand for their products increased, provided the price of the product of the innovating industry is flexible. This will in all probability be the case also with an elasticity of one and possibly with an elasticity of more than one, but not so evidently. If we consider only the matter of price elasticity, other industries would be unaffected with an elasticity of one, and they would suffer a decline in demand with an elasticity of more than one. However, we must also consider the effect of the increased incomes of the owners of the innovating industry. The demand of these owners will probably exhibit some income elasticity for the products of other industries; and if so, then there will clearly be an increased total demand for the products of other industries, even though the (price) elasticity of demand for the product of the innovating industry is unitary. This increased demand for the products of other industries on the part of the owners of the innovating industry might or might not offset the decrease in demand for those products on the part of others if the price elasticity of demand for the product of the innovating industry were more than one. It is clearly possible that the amount demanded of each individual product should rise; but even if this should occur, it would still be true that a reallocation of the labor force would be required.

If some degree of monopoly prevailed in the innovating industry, there would probably also be some measure of price inflexibility. To be sure, if there were a complete monopoly, and if the monopolist were guided exclusively by the profit-maximizing principle of equality between marginal cost and marginal revenue, an innovation would result in a prompt decline in price, since it would reduce marginal cost. Furthermore, under these conditions the elasticity of demand would always be more than one, inasmuch as a monopolist will fix output so that the price falls within an elastic segment of the demand curve—again, if he is guided solely by the criterion of equality between marginal cost and marginal revenue. Under conditions of pure monopoly, therefore, and with rigorous exclusion of all considerations other than that of immediate maximization of monopoly profit, the monopolist would reduce his price with improving technology, the demand for the products of other industries would fall and consequently also employment (ignoring now the effect of a possible increase in demand on the part of the owners of the innovating industry). Employment would therefore rise in the innovating (monopolized) industry.

However, fear of potential competition and of adverse public reaction might deter even a complete monopoly from rigorously following the policy of equating marginal cost and marginal revenue. Furthermore, monopolists seem to feel that in some way it is praiseworthy to maintain a stable price for their products. For these reasons a monopoly might not so promptly reduce prices as costs went down as was assumed in the preceding paragraph. In any case, oligopoly is more frequently encountered than complete and uncontrolled monopoly, and price is likely to be fully as inflexible under conditions of some form of partial monopoly as under pure monopoly. It is conceivable that it should be more so. Moreover, under oligopolistic conditions there is no assurance that output will be so fixed that price will fall within an elastic segment of the demand curve.

Rigidity of the price of the product will always increase the extent of the required reallocation of resources in the case of a shift in demand; but while this will probably be true also in the case of an innovation, it will not necessarily be so. If the product price is rigid, resources will flow out of the innovating industry regardless of the degree of elasticity of demand, since output will be unchanged, but a smaller amount of resources will be required than formerly for this level of output. This means that the outflow that *would* have occurred under conditions of price flexibility and elasticity of less than one, the outflow that *probably* would have occurred with an elasticity of one, and the outflow that *might* have occurred with an elasticity of more than one would be accentuated. In place of an inflow that might have occurred with an elasticity of more than one, there would be an outflow. There is no way of knowing whether the reversal of the direction of the flow in the last case would lead to a larger or a smaller transfer of resources (in the opposite direction) than would be required with flexible prices.

If the price of the product of the innovating industry were rigid, flexibility of wage rates in that industry would be of little assistance in avoiding frictional unemployment. Workers must leave the industry in any case, although a reduction in wage rates might to some extent induce the owners to substitute labor for other ingredients of production, and thus to a minor extent reduce the necessary exodus of workers from the industry.

If, however, the product prices are flexible (and if there is not a high degree of homogeneity and mobility in the labor force), flexibility of wage rates becomes a matter of major importance. A reduction in rates of pay in the innovating industry (in the usual case of a required outflow of workers from the industry) would further reduce costs and the price of the product, thus minimizing the number of workers that would be immediately expelled from the industry. The reduction in wage rates would, of course, be only temporary if the impediments to mobility were eventually overcome. In the less likely case of a required flow of workers into the innovating industry, the required reduction in wage rates (which would now come in the noninnovating industries) would be very small, since the number of workers forced to leave the other industries would be small relative to the total number of workers in those industries. The smaller the proportion of wages to total variable costs, the greater will need to be the wage reduction if employment is to be maintained by means of a wage reduction alone. Moreover, since raw materials are generally used in numerous industries, and since the amount used in the innovating industry will probably increase, their prices will usually not decline.

In the absence of a very high degree of mobility of labor, perhaps higher than in practice could ever be achieved, it is manifest that product prices and wage rates must exhibit a considerable amount of flexibility if frictional unemployment is not to be unduly large. It is equally evident, moreover, that in some cases the extent of the required wage reduction might be drastic.

It may be objected that the preceding analysis of the effect of innovations will hold only if the improvement is labor saving. It is true that the direction and extent of the shift in the labor force might be different if the innovation were not of this character, but the likelihood that it will not be is remote. If an advance in technology is not labor saving, it must mean that in the combined use and production of the equipment of an industry no less labor is required for a given level of final output than before the improvement. This could be true only if the new machines, while more efficient, were less complicated and therefore less costly to produce than the old ones, and if the lower cost of production were itself due to a reduced capital requirement in the equipment-producing industry, rather than to a lessened amount of labor. Such developments are highly improbable. They are, in fact, precisely contrary to the usual consequences of an innovation.

Even though the preceding discussion is by no means exhaustive, it is ample to demonstrate the very minor role of monetary policy in reducing frictional unemployment. An announced monetary policy which indirectly had the effect of maintaining aggregate demand would prevent a radical decline in money income if a reallocation of the labor force on a large scale were required and could not be achieved in a sufficiently short period of time to prevent a high level of unemployment. In this instance, monetary policy, therefore, would prevent the conversion of truly frictional unemployment into a yet larger volume of general unemployment brought on by a decline in aggregate demand. This means, to put the same point in different words, that where workers were required to leave a given industry, monetary policy would give assurance of rising demand in other industries, and thus the shifting of workers would be facilitated.[1]

III

A third type of unemployment is possible if labor monopolies are so extensive that no open segments of the economy remain to absorb those forced out of work in the mo-

[1] The problem of depressed areas is a difficult one. If an important export industry for a given locality loses a large part of its outside demand, if labor has little mobility, and if wage rates are inflexible, unemployment on a major scale will be the consequence. If wage rates are flexible, and if the occupation which has the next highest productivity after that which has lost its market is, nevertheless, far below the latter in effectiveness, the consequence will be a drastic decline in the standard of living. It may be that the price system will do little or nothing to remedy conditions of this kind, since the factors impeding mobility may be much too strong to be overcome by wage differentials between the region in question and other regions.

In general, the position of a nineteenth-century liberal "ought" to be in favor of free international, as well as intranational, movement of persons; and yet this position cannot be taken so completely without exception as can one in defense of free movement of goods. The reasons for desiring free trade and freedom of movement for persons are quite different. In the one case it is that of maximizing the material well-being of all peoples; in the other it is that of extending individual freedom. Movement of population from densely populated areas of low living standards and high death rates to regions of high standards is likely to have no effect whatever upon standards in emigrant areas, but it may well reduce standards in regions of immigration. A liberal policy requires freedom of movement among nations in which population is kept in check by a low birth rate. Nations which are unwilling to impose this check may not rightly demand the privilege of free entry for their citizens into other regions.

nopolized occupations. Under these circumstances underemployment of a nonfrictional kind would become chronic.

If we assume that all laborers are organized in monopolistic unions, which force wage rates above the marginal productivity of the workers under conditions of full employment, the consequence must be general unemployment, whether or not industry is competitive. As wage rates are forced up, employers will reduce output in an effort to equalize marginal cost and marginal revenue, and there will be no reservoir of opportunities for employment to absorb workers forced out of work in the monopolized occupations, since there will be no occupation in which rates of pay can be reduced. It might be contended that the quantity of money was inadequate to allow product prices to rise to a level that would permit full employment at existing costs of production; but an attempt to remedy the situation by means of an increase in the quantity of money, and consequently a rise in product prices, would lead to renewed demands by the labor monopolies for increases in wage rates. The unions would point out that, since the cost of living had risen, "justice" required that wage rates rise correspondingly. So long, therefore, as the labor monopolies maintained their power, any attempt to maintain employment by means of monetary action would result in continuously rising prices, to say nothing of the chronic industrial warfare as an incidental part of the whole process.

Furthermore, the increase in wage rates imposed upon industry by the labor monopolies would reduce the rate of return on existing equipment, as well as the expected return on new investment. There would also be full knowledge on the part of potential investors of the power of the labor monopolies to raise wage rates to still higher levels, and thus to reduce further the rate of return on investment. Consequently new investment would be discouraged. When such conditions had arisen, the public would doubtless be told that opportunities for investment were insufficient to provide full employment, and that a large volume of public investment was required. And who could deny the absence of "opportunities"?

The effects of widespread product monopolies would be significantly different from those of equally extensive labor monopolies, since they could not, as would complete labor monopolies, include the activities rendering personal services. Therefore, as product prices were raised, output decreased, and the number of workers reduced in the monopolized industries, the evicted workers could find employment in personal-service activities of one kind or another, granted a free labor market in those occupations. Given flexible wage rates, there would need be no chronic unemployment directly traceable to the monopolies, although the rigidity of product prices would promote purely frictional unemployment in the absence of a high degree of mobility of labor. Wage rates would be forced below the level that would prevail in a generally competitive economy in the occupations rendering personal services. The monopolists themselves would therefore be able to obtain workers (in a free labor market) at rates of pay lower than employers would have been required to pay under competitive conditions in product markets.

While product monopolies, in so far as they maintain rigid prices, tend to increase frictional unemployment, it is probable that their more marked effects are on the distribution of income. To find in a monopoly-ridden country a relatively small number of very wealthy persons and at the same time a large proportion of the population living in poverty would be a normal expectation. Nevertheless, there would need be no reason why aggregate demand should be insufficient to maintain employment at a high level. To be sure, the output of the country would consist of genuine luxury goods to a marked extent. By "genuine" luxury goods I refer to those commodities which are purchased by the wealthy only, as distinguished from certain articles which are widely consumed by the lower income groups but which are, nevertheless, frequently and with doubtful propriety referred to as luxuries. A country which relies largely upon the exports of a single industry for its national income would afford an excellent opportunity for this disparity of income to develop if its one important industry should become monopolized.[2]

IV

Frictional unemployment and chronic unemployment because of the extensive development of labor monopolies are not susceptible to control by monetary measures, although monetary stability would furnish the framework within which direct attacks on these problems would work out most effectively. Possibly a small amount of inflation would reduce frictional unemployment somewhat, and yet this is unlikely. A stable price level holds promise of yielding results equally good in this respect, and it would avoid unfortunate effects on those having fixed incomes. Furthermore, stable monetary conditions guided by any reasonable criterion would avoid any marked decline in aggregate demand that might otherwise eventuate from changes of great magnitude in the economy and would thus limit the resulting unemployment to the genuinely frictional kind.

The only way in which monetary action might relieve chronic unemployment growing out of extensive labor mo-

[2] It is unlikely that the above extreme cases of either labor or product monopolies could be developed in practice without active governmental support. If the government rigorously kept hands off, the result undoubtedly would be that many industries and occupations would be controlled by strong monopolies, while other segments of the economy, being less susceptible to the application of restrictive measures, would continue to be competitive. The consequence would be a high level of frictional unemployment, great disparity of income (even within the working class), industrial warfare, and in effect collusion between associations of workers and employers, as well as within such associations, to exploit that part of the public which did not have membership in some "protected" group.

nopolies would come from a product price level constantly rising one step ahead of wage rates. Thus, at best, any attempt to reduce this type of unemployment by monetary measures would lead to an unending race between the monetary agency and the labor unions, with inflation and constant industrial warfare as the inevitable result. Moreover, it is by no means clear that unemployment would actually be reduced in any significant measure, since it cannot be presumed that the labor unions would be unaware of what was happening, or that they would fail to take action to eliminate the typical lag in wage rates behind product prices during periods of inflation.

It should be noted, further, that monetary stability might itself be of some aid in opposing the growth of monopolies, both product and labor. It is during periods of serious decline in output and employment that the incentive for the introduction of "protective" restrictions is strongest. Whether this effect substantially increases the strength of monopolies or merely brings about variations in the extent of their power or in their rate of growth, is uncertain.[3]

[3] It is anomalous that humanitarians should in preponderant numbers look upon union control of wage rates as an effective means of bringing about the kind of redistribution of income which they desire. To be sure, "successful" unions decrease the income of the employer and increase that of their own members who retain their jobs; but they also increase the number of workers in the open occupations and consequently reduce their rates of pay. The redistributive effect, therefore, is not merely that of reducing the income of the employer for the benefit of the workers; it also increases the disparity of income *within* the working class. An increase in income differentials can thus as reasonably be said to be the final effect as a decrease in them. Whether union action also operates to decrease the aggregate output of the community is an unanswerable question. Certainly in the unionized occupations output will be decreased, but it will be increased in the open occupations. The character of output will, therefore, be so changed as to render the two magnitudes imcomparable.

Chapter 3

THE PROPENSITY TO HOARD AND UNEMPLOYMENT

I

I shall use the term "propensity to hoard" to indicate the extent of the demand for money to hold as a cash balance on the part of individuals, business firms, and any other holders of cash. It manifestly must be measured in real terms of some kind, but more precisely what this measure should be is not of present interest. There are many reasons for a change in this propensity; but whatever the reason, the consequence is a change in the level of employment and output in the absence of a stabilizing monetary policy. Unemployment growing out of a rise in the propensity to hoard is, therefore, a monetary phenomenon, both in the sense that the proximate cause is a change in the velocity of circulation of money and in the sense that monetary action could at least greatly reduce the extent of such unemployment. Currently the stagnation theorists attach an even greater importance to the propensity to hoard. They hold that not only do changes in this propensity lead to fluctuations in employment, but that probably in the near future an unduly high propensity to hoard will obtain, and that this fact will result in chronic unemployment of a nonfrictional kind unless deliberate steps are taken to prevent such a development.

There is no single immediate effect that must be assumed

as the consequence of a change in the propensity to hoard. The disturbance that causes the change may, according to its nature, initially affect the expectations and actions of either one group or another. Furthermore, an increase, for example, in the demand for cash on the part of a given individual may be at the expense of any one or more of several ways in which he might have disposed of his income. These possibilities are as follows:

1. Purchase of consumers' goods.
2. Purchase of producers' goods.
3. Lend on short term.
4. Purchase of long-term bonds.
5. Purchase of corporation shares.

If, for example, an increased demand for cash affects the demand for producers' goods only, we should then expect the prices of such goods immediately to decline and unemployment to result in the producers' goods industries. If, however, it affects only the demand for long-term bonds, in the first instance we should expect bond prices to fall, which is the same thing as a rise in the rate of interest. This would lead to a decline in investment. In either case we should have the beginning of a decline in employment that could reach unpredictable proportions. If we have the temerity to generalize either of these assumptions or others that might be made, to the effect that an increased propensity to hoard always produces this initial effect and only this, we can go on to construct imposing and quite divergent theories concerning the consequences of changes in the demand for cash.

II

Say's so-called law to the effect that production creates its own demand and that, therefore, there can be no general overproduction is a convenient point of departure for a discussion of fluctuations in employment which grow out of variations in the propensity to hoard.[1] Production does, indeed, create sufficient income to take the aggregate of commodities off the market at prices which cover the costs producers have actually incurred and therefore enough income to maintain output. Whether there will be a general decline in output at any given time depends (granting there is no disequilibrating increase in costs) upon the degree of stability in the rate of expenditure of income for commodities and services—upon the degree of stability in the velocity of circulation of money and upon the absence of inappropriate changes in the stock of money. Say unwarrantedly contended both that producers would be equally anxious at all times to sell their product, and that income receivers would never for long postpone the purchase of commodities after the receipt of their income. He referred to the possibility of a decline in the value of money as a reason for spending income promptly; but he failed to mention that a rise in the value of money is also possible, and that the expectation of such a development might cause the public to refrain from spending. The truth of the matter is that the willingness to spend varies for many reasons and, when it declines, prices, output, employment,

[1] "It is worth while to remark, that a product is no sooner created, than it, from that instant, affords a market for other products to the full extent of its own value. When the producer has put the finishing hand to his product, he is most anxious to sell it immediately, lest its value should diminish in his hands. Nor is he less anxious to dispose of the money he may get for it; for the value of money is also perishable. But the only way of getting rid of money is in the purchase of some product or other. Thus, the mere circumstance of the creation of one product immediately opens a vent for other products.

"But it may be asked, if this be so, how does it happen, that there is at times so great a glut of commodities in the market, and so much difficulty in finding a vent for them? I answer that the glut of a particular commodity arises from its having outrun the total demand for it in one of two ways; either because it has been produced in excessive abundance, or because the production of other commodities has fallen short." [J. B. Say, *A Treatise on Political Economy,* translated by C. R. Prinsep (6th American ed., 1834), pp. 138–139.]

and business profits fall. "Spending" is here assumed to include the purchase of producers' goods.

The impact of an increase in the propensity to hoard will depend upon what group it is that first develops pessimistic expectations. In some cases it might be the owners of productive enterprises; in others, the speculators; and conceivably, in yet other cases, it might even be the consumers. More probably all these classes will be affected in some measure. If the initial change in expectations comes in only one group, it is most likely to be the producers. Speculators are highly sensitive to changes in conditions, and they are likely to react in a more decisive manner than other persons do; yet the owners of enterprises themselves are most likely to be the first to obtain the information that constitutes the basis for a change in expectations. However, many individuals are members of two, or even all three, of these groups, and any forebodings they may have about the future are likely to cause them to react in all of their several capacities.

There is great unwillingness to reduce one's standard of living; yet this fact does not preclude the possibility that an attempt to increase cash balances may be at the expense of a reduction in the purchase of consumers' goods. In modern life there are many durable consumers' goods, and their useful life is elastic. One can continue to run an old automobile for a while longer, even though it be noisy and unattractive in appearance, and though the maintenance costs be high. It seems perfectly reasonable to suppose that a decline in the demand for durable consumers' goods should be one of the initial effects of an increase in the propensity to hoard, although it is not so likely to be the *only* immediate consequence of such a development. If, nevertheless, this should occur, output and prices of these goods would decline, and failing an increase in the quantity of money, income would fall. As a secondary consequence, investment would be reduced and the whole cumulative process of a depression would be under way. One of the secondary effects would be the decline in marginal productivity and, consequently, of the rate of interest. However, the decline in output would not be likely to be severe if there were no aggravating decrease in the stock of money.

If businessmen become apprehensive about the future, they will be reluctant to undertake expansions of capacity or to start new enterprises. Consequently investment and income will decline, and again we have the beginning of the cumulative process, granting no offsetting increase in the stock of money. There will be no increase in the rate of interest at any stage of the process. On the contrary, as the depression deepens, the marginal productivity of capital will progressively decline and, consequently, also the rate of interest.

Both in the case of a decline in the demand for consumers' goods and in that for producers' goods, any change in the rate of interest is consequential rather than causal. If the difficulty starts with consumers' goods, the sequence will be more or less as follows: a decline in the output and prices of consumers' goods; then a decline, concurrently, in investment, income, and the rate of interest; and next a continued decline in the demand for consumers' goods. If the downturn starts with producers' goods, the first step in this sequence will be omitted. Expectations are likely to become constantly more adverse for a period of time.

Misgivings about the future may possibly arise first among investors and speculators, who as a consequence will be desirous of increasing the amount of their cash holdings at the current rates of interest. In this case the initial impact of the increased demand for cash may be on bond prices, which will go down. However, the doubts about the future will quickly spread. There will undoubtedly be a decline in investment and income, but more from the general growth of pessimism than from the rise in the rate of interest. The forces of the depression will take charge of the interest rate. The marginal productivity of capital will be reduced because of depressed business conditions, the demand for funds will decline, the rate of interest will fall, and a continued rise in the propensity to hoard or a decrease in the quantity of money will serve further indirectly to depress the rate. As income declines, we again have the cumulative forces of the depression in operation. While in this case the immediate effect of the increased propensity to hoard is on the rate of interest, nevertheless, the rise of the rate is only transitory.

It may be that for some individuals the quantity of money held (in real terms) is a function of the rate of interest, but it does not follow that the rate is determined by the demand for money for hoarding purposes, nor, therefore, that an increase in this demand will raise the rate. We have three factors to be kept in equilibrium: the quantity of money, the rate of interest, and the general price level. If the rate is at such a level that those holders of cash who are influenced by the rate desire to hold more than they have, then the price level, employment, marginal productivity, and the rate of interest will all decline, and at some point a new equilibrium will be established; but at all times during these developments (except possibly immediately after a change or during a crisis) the rate of interest will be determined independently of the quantity of money and the level of liquidity preferences; except that it will be *temporarily* and *indirectly* reduced by an increase in liquidity preferences, since the decrease in output will have reduced marginal productivity.

There is no logical end to these developments short of complete cessation of economic activity if the quantity of money is so determined that it can decrease with zero only as the limit. Actually, of course, there is some indefinite minimum below which even modern perversely elastic moneys cannot be reduced, and when this level has been reached any further decline in the level of prices will raise the volume of cash balances in real terms. When these conditions obtain, it will not be long before the public will at the worst demand a sufficient volume of goods to stop the decline in prices, rather than to permit their cash balances to continue to rise. If this point is reached with a low level of output, the rate of interest will have been reduced by the decline in the marginal productivity of capital, and those holders of cash who are influenced by the rate will have adjusted their cash holdings to the rate as they find it.

This is not to say that, if the current rate of interest is so low as to produce a speculative demand for funds to be hoarded that is in excess of the money available to meet this demand, equilibrium will be reached at a still lower rate, although this is indeed a possibility. Under such conditions the absorption of cash to meet the speculative demand will cause prices to go down, and the consequent rise in the real value of cash balances will meet the demand for larger cash balances. After the temporarily adverse effects on employment and marginal productivity are a thing of the past, the rate of interest will return to its former level; unless wage rates cannot be reduced, in which case equilibrium will be achieved without the return to full employment and at a *lower* rate of interest than formerly prevailed. The total demand of the community for cash (in monetary terms) is primarily a function of the value of money and of the level of real income, with the rate of interest a matter of decidedly minor importance. Consequently, only a slight decline in prices will release amounts of cash that are large relative to the total demand of those few who may be influenced by the rate.

If a panic develops, the desire on the part of businessmen to protect themselves against unforeseeable contingencies by having a plentiful stock of cash on hand may lead them actually to borrow funds to be hoarded. If this should occur, the short-term rate will rise, but this rise will be only temporary. A more enduring effect of a rise in the desire to hold cash will be that on the rate on high-grade, short-term, credit instruments. Investments in these near-moneys will serve to some extent to satisfy the demand for cash, and they have the great advantage of yielding some income. Consequently, except during panic, the demand for them during depression is likely to rise, with a resulting decline in their yield, both absolutely and relatively to the yield on long-term bonds.

The behavior of rates from 1929 to 1933, inclusive, is consistent with the above analysis. The New York rates on prime commercial paper and bankers' acceptances were at the same levels in October, 1929 (the month of the stock-market panic), as in the preceding month, but they began to fall in November. The yield on high-grade corporate bonds also fell, but not so markedly. Thereafter all of these rates declined almost continuously until the autumn of 1931, at which time they all rose sharply. It will be remembered that it was in September of this year that Great Britain left the gold standard, and there was fear that the United States would be compelled to do likewise. The conditions were those of near panic at best. Throughout 1932 all these rates were declining, except for a rise during some three or four months in the first half of the year in the yield on bonds. All again rose sharply during the banking panic in the spring of 1933, but again very quickly declined. To be sure, many individual bonds declined greatly in price during these years, but these declines were the result of the progressive worsening of the credit standing of the issuers. Such concerns were simply out of the market as borrowers, and the high yield on their previously issued bonds is no indication whatever of the current level of interest rates.

III

Why have depressions become cumulatively worse for a considerable period of time? Or why is it that there have not been automatic responses to a decline in employment which would bring the system promptly back to a position of equilibrium and "full" employment? There are these three possible reasons: (1) the perverse behavior of the stock of money; (2) the development of adverse expectations, which themselves are based on the absence of any stabilizing monetary policy; and (3) rigidity of wage rates. The first of these factors is, without much doubt, the primary reason; the second is itself derived from public knowledge of the prevalence of the first; and the third has probably been of secondary importance at most.

Both because of the inherent instability of an uncontrolled fractional-reserve banking system and of the absence of any intelligent governmental monetary policy, a serious decline in employment has typically been accompanied by a reduction in the quantity of circulating medium. In fact, it is quite possible that in some instances a decline in the stock of money has been the initiating factor in bringing on depressions, as well as an aggravating factor after the decline has been started.[2] The behavior of the stock of money, the price level, and industrial production during periods of declining output since 1920 are as shown in Table 1.

Undoubtedly, the failure of the quantity of money to decline in 1923 to 1924 and the very slight decline in 1927 were both a cause and a consequence of the mildness of the recession in business activity. In so far as they were a cause, the Federal Reserve Board may well deserve the credit, since it made an effort in these two periods to prevent the decline. It would be my guess, however, that the primary reason for the failure of a major depression to develop was an absence of any seriously disturbing factors.

[2] Clark Warburton contends that the initiating factor in depressions has been a failure of the stock of money to increase equivalently with the "need" for money, "need" being measured by the growth in transactions and the increase in the demand for liquid resources. This failure of the stock of money to increase sufficiently has brought on a decline in prices, so he contends, and this in turn has ushered in the depression. To me Warburton's evidence seems inconclusive, which is equivalent to saying that he may be right. See his "Monetary Theory, Full Production, and the Great Depression," *Econometrica,* XIII (1945), 114–128.

TABLE 1. THE QUANTITY OF MONEY, PRICES, AND INDUSTRIAL PRODUCTION DURING RECENT PERIODS OF DECLINING OUTPUT

Year	Deposits and currency as of June 30, billions *	Index of wholesale prices (1926 = 100) †		Index of industrial Production (1935–1939 = 100) ‡	
		June	Months of peaks and troughs	June	Months of peaks and troughs
1920	$23.7	167	167 (June)	79	82 (February)
1921	20.8	93	91 (January, 1922)	57	55 (March)
1923	22.7	100	105 (March)	91	92 (May)
1924	23.1	95	95 (June)	77	75 (July)
1926	25.6	101	105 (November, 1925)	95	98 (October)
1927	25.5	94	94 (April)	97	92 (October)
1929	26.2	95	99 (September, 1928)	114	114 (August)
1933	19.2	65	60 (February)	78	53 (July, 1932)
1937	30.7	87	88 (April)	119	121 (May)
1938	29.8	78	75 (August, 1939)	81	80 (May)

* Board of Governors of the Federal Reserve System, *Banking and Monetary Statistics* (1943), pp. 34–35. The figures include demand deposits adjusted and currency outside banks. United States government deposits are excluded. The table gives the peak and trough figures for each period, except the peaks preceding the declines in output in 1929 and 1937, and the trough for the depression of 1937–1938. These figures were $26.7, $31.0, and $29.6 billion; and they came in December, 1928; December, 1936; and December, 1937, respectively.

† *Annual Report of the Federal Reserve Board* (1927), pp. 127–129; *ibid.*, 1933, p. 251; *Federal Reserve Bulletin*, XXIV (1938), 53; *ibid.*, XXVI (1940), 979. The index numbers are those of the Bureau of Labor Statistics. In some instances the highs and lows of a period were reached in more than one month. In such cases the latest high and the earliest low are given in the table.

‡ *Federal Reserve Bulletin*, XXVI (1940), 764–765. The index numbers are those of the Federal Reserve Board. In some instances the highs and lows of a period were reached in more than one month. In such cases the latest high and the earliest low are given in the table.

The Board's action in 1929 and the early 1930's does not support a presumption that it would have done much to combat a serious disturbance in the earlier years.

In the other three periods of depression shown in the table there was a significant decline in the quantity of money and a drastic decline in industrial production. To permit the volume of money to vary in this manner reflects a tragic failure in the management of our monetary affairs. Nevertheless, many economists would presumably approve of the decline in bank deposits, since they hold that bank loans are, or ought to be, made only to finance bona fide business transactions, and that the rise and fall of the volume of deposits comes only in response to the "needs of business."

A second reason for the prolongation of a period of low or declining output will arise if businessmen develop adverse expectations in consequence of the prevailing conditions. Let us assume that industry is composed exclusively of small producers, each of whom produces for the market and employs no workers.[3] If the price of his product declines, but only equivalently with that of all other goods, including the raw materials he uses, it is clear that the producer will suffer no loss of real income by maintaining his output. Even though his product brings less than the materials have cost him, his real income will still not decline if he maintains his output, since his lower money income will purchase as much, in raw materials and consumers' goods, as formerly. Nevertheless, it does not follow that this situation cannot lead to unemployment. Unless each producer buys raw materials only as he produces—that is, unless he carries no stocks of materials—it will be possible for him to continue his production for a time without purchasing any additional materials. Precisely this he will be tempted to do if he anticipates that a prevailingly downward trend in prices

[3] This illustrative example is borrowed, but somewhat changed, from Alfred and Mary Paley Marshall, *The Economics of Industry* (2d ed., 1881), pp. 155–156. See also *Official Papers by Alfred Marshall,* J. M. Keynes, ed., (1926), pp. 7–8.

will continue, even though he expects all prices to fall at the same rate; since he will hope, not to avoid a loss, but to obtain a speculative gain.

If each of our small producers stays off the market in the hope of getting his material at a better price, this will lead to an immediate reduction of output by those among them who produce semifinished or raw materials and who are unwilling to increase the stocks of their products. Moreover, they will in fact be more desirous of reducing these stocks than of increasing them, since prices are falling. The decreased sales of this group will almost certainly reduce their purchases also, and the repercussions will thus spread throughout industry, leading to a progressively greater amount of unemployment, even though the instruments of production are exclusively operated by their owners. Doubtless in so simple an economy, reduction of output would never proceed to such depths as it does today. Nevertheless, this simple illustration does reveal an important force which is likely to develop and *for a time* to aggravate a downward trend in prices and output.

While expectations may in the above-explained manner have a part in magnifying fluctuations in output, we should nevertheless be cautious in our attempts to appraise this factor. Businessmen are as aware that a given trend in prices has been reversed in the past as that it has continued for a time. Even though they may in some measure act upon the assumption that the existing trend will continue, it is equally clear that at some time they will reverse their expectations. Furthermore, and this is the important consideration, it is the monetary instability which both justifies to some extent the expectation of the continuance of price changes in a given direction and renders it difficult to evaluate the forces that will reverse the trend. If a policy of monetary stabilization prevailed, the general expectation would be, not that an existing upward or downward trend in prices would or might continue, but that it would very quickly cease and possibly be reversed. But further than this, the emergence in the first place of adverse expectations in any significant degree would be improbable. In actual practice during the last century and a half, the strength of these expectations has undoubtedly been derived from the lack of any explicit monetary policy, in consequence of which the stock of money has so changed as to accentuate, for a time, any existing trend. Recently too much consideration has been given to the question of adverse expectations, and not enough to the monetary instability on which they are founded or to the monetary measures that might be taken to avoid them. In brief, a policy of monetary stabilization would transform expectations from a frequently destabilizing factor into a prevailingly stabilizing influence of the first importance.

A third reason for the failure of periods of declining output to end more quickly is to be found in the rigidity of wage rates. The debate on this question has too frequently been carried on without explicit reference to monetary conditions. Any such discussion is futile. It may well be that a general reduction of wage rates at a time of falling prices and declining output will be of little or no help if monetary conditions are such that the stock of money tends spontaneously to fall with worsening business conditions. These are the circumstances that have prevailed in the past and that have been too often implicitly assumed by those who deny the efficacy of flexible wages in promoting a high level of employment. The conclusion is then drawn that a reduction of wage rates is ineffective, without consideration of the alternative conclusion that perverse monetary conditions are the root of the difficulty. Under conditions of monetary stability, a change in wage rates is no more likely to give rise to disequilibrating expectations than is a decline or fall in the general price level.

Under a combination of the gold standard, fractional-reserve banking, and an absence of any explicit monetary policy on the part of the government, it is likely that the quantity of money will decrease for a considerable period of time after a decline in employment sets in, but that it will ultimately reach some ill-defined minimum. When this minimum has been reached, the real value of cash balances will rise with further decreases in the price level. When these conditions prevailed, a reduction in wage rates would without much doubt increase employment. During past periods of declining employment it seems likely that, for much of the time, conditions were such that a wage reduction would have been of no aid in increasing employment; but that at long last such reductions may have been of some assistance. However, in any case reliance upon this final stabilization of the stock of money under unstable monetary conditions and wage reductions is a woefully and unnecessarily slow means of combatting depression.

It is only because of the perverse behavior of the stock of money that conditions ever arise in which there can be doubt as to the effect of reductions in wage rates. Furthermore, with a reasonable monetary policy, there would never be any need of a *general* reduction of wage rates. Under such conditions the chief value of flexible wage rates would be in reducing the level of frictional unemployment.

IV

The stagnation theorists look upon the propensity to hoard as a probable source of a more serious difficulty than that of fluctuations in output. While they profess belief in the desirability of private enterprise, they assert that, if we are to maintain a high level of employment and to avoid collectivization of the economy, we shall be compelled to resort to large and possibly highly variable expenditures by the central government. They contend that Western nations have now reached a position wherein the propensity to save will be such, with incomes that result from "full" employment, that the opportunities for private investment will be insufficient to absorb all of these savings. That is to say, at rates of interest low enough to induce a sufficient volume of investment, savers will prefer in considerable measure to hoard cash rather than to lend their savings.

The stagnationists assert, in support of their contentions, that on the one hand the wealth of the Western nations and its highly unequal distribution result in a relatively low propensity to consume; while on the other hand, of the opportunities for investment which were provided during the nineteenth century by technological advances, the development of new lands, and the growth of population, only the first of these will remain, since no new lands will be available and population will become stable in the relatively near future. The industrial nations, so runs the argument, are too wealthy for their own highest welfare. They now have so large an accumulation of capital that technological advances alone will not open up a sufficient volume of investment opportunities to absorb, at rates of interest which are feasible, the total amount that would be saved with "full" employment.

If, for example, the net national income would be $200 billion under conditions of "full" employment, and if under these conditions $40 billion would be saved but only $20 billion privately invested, the conclusion seems superficially inescapable that a high level of employment could not be had without $20 billion of public investment. Indeed, the stagnationists conclude that if the public investment were financed by taxation it might require more than $20 billion, since the taxes would reduce to some extent consumption and private investment.

While I disagree with the stagnationists in their appraisal of conditions, it must be conceded that conclusive evidence of the incorrectness of their estimates cannot be presented; but it is equally true that their position cannot be established by any of the available evidence. Nevertheless, there are some facts which bear on the problem and which tend to cast doubt upon the stagnation theories.

Essentially the difference of opinion as to the volume of investment opportunities rests upon conflicting interpretations of the low level of employment during the 1930's. The stagnation theorists have too quickly concluded that the circumstances of the thirties reflect the emergence of inevitably permanent conditions making for unemployment.[4] They have come to this conclusion, I believe, without adequate consideration of the possible reasons for the low level of employment during these years.

In the United States neither the Federal government nor the Federal Reserve System did anything of substantial importance until the spring of 1932 to combat the depression which began in the autumn of 1929. To be sure, the Reserve System gradually reduced its rediscount rates and its buying rate on bills, but nevertheless it did not take positive action, through open-market purchases, to offset the decline in the stock of money and in velocity that were taking place. In effect, both the Reserve System and the government took passive positions on the side lines (the former until 1932, and the latter until 1933) and allowed employment and output to proceed on their disastrous downward courses unhindered. The total earning assets of the Reserve banks at

[4] See, for example, Oscar Lange, "Is the American Economy Contracting?" *American Economic Review,* XXIX (1939), 503–513. In this article Lange gives statistical data of various kinds to show the decline in income and employment during the 1930's, assuming without argument that such data reveal a tendency toward secular stagnation. On the last page he does, indeed, say that "the trend is largely due to the severity of the depression," and, two paragraphs later, that "any prediction as to the future of economic expansion in the United States can be made only on the basis of a knowledge of the causes which stopped economic expansion since 1929 and of the expectation as to whether, and in what degree, these causes are likely to persist in the future." These are reasonable statements, but the next sentence after the second of these runs as follows: "The events since 1929 in the United States and in other countries with an advanced industrial capitalism show that private capitalism suffers from a lack of sufficient inducements to invest which prevent it from securing full employment of the existing productive resources." I am unable to understand how Lange gets from the first and second of these statements to the third.

specified dates were as given in Table 2. Indexes of the wholesale price level and of industrial production are included, to facilitate comparisons.

TABLE 2. EARNING ASSETS OF FEDERAL RESERVE BANKS, PRICES, AND PRODUCTION *

Date	Earning assets, millions	Wholesale price index (1926 = 100)	Index of industrial production (1923–1925 = 100)
July, 1929	$1,380	96.5	120
October, 1929	1,450	95.1	121
December, 1929	1,643	93.3	96
March, 1930	1,095	90.2	106
July, 1931	954	72.0	80
October, 1931	2,088	70.3	75
March, 1932	1,652	66.0	68
July, 1932	2,422	64.5	56
February, 1933	2,224	59.8	64
December, 1933	2,669	70.8	69

* *Annual Report of the Federal Reserve Board* (1933), pp. 74–75, 240–241, 251. The index of wholesale prices is that of the Bureau of Labor Statistics; that of industrial production is that of the Federal Reserve Board.

Between December, 1929, and July, 1931, during which time prices and output were almost continuously declining, the earning assets of the Reserve banks declined by 42 per cent. It may be conceded that we do not have complete assurance that the Reserve System has the power by itself to stabilize the price level or to achieve alone any other goal of monetary policy that might be stipulated; but what power the system does have could have been thrown in the right direction, whereas it was in fact placed substantially on the side of deflation. The defenders of the system will doubtless answer that its reluctance to expand the volume of its credit was founded upon a feeling of responsibility for maintaining the convertibility of the currency. To this defense there is a sufficient answer. It was the worsening of business conditions, with its concomitant effect on the banks, that was endangering the gold standard; and a restrictive monetary policy was well suited to make these conditions worse. Fundamentally there can be no conflict between the requirement for monetary stability and that for maintaining convertibility during a crisis, although this is not to say that in all cases the effort to stabilize monetary conditions will result in avoidance of a suspension of specie payments. It can only be said that a narrow concentration on the problem of maintaining convertibility is less likely to achieve this end than would be an outright attempt to achieve general monetary stability. Furthermore, had there been in effect, in the autumn of 1929, an adequately implemented policy of monetary stabilization, the occasions for the restrictive measures of the Reserve officials to maintain convertibility would never have arisen.[5]

The officials of the government likewise failed to take positive and adequate remedial action. Virtually no monetary measures were taken by the government to combat the depression before 1933. Indeed, for the year 1930 there was a very small surplus of receipts over expenditures. When a deficit spontaneously appeared in 1931 it was widely "viewed with alarm," and the successor to President Hoover proclaimed, during the presidential campaign of 1932, that if he were elected he would balance the budget! In contending that such action was desirable, he was merely echoing a prevailing point of view. At the instigation of President Hoover, the National Credit Corporation was organized in the autumn of 1931, and the Glass-Steagal Act was passed in February, 1932; but these measures were both inadequate

[5] I intend that my criticisms of the Reserve System shall be unambiguous and largely adverse; but I do not mean to imply that another group of men, under the same conditions and operating with the same grant of discretionary power, would have done better. It is to discretionary monetary authorities that I object; and the unwise actions of any particular group of men possessed of such powers constitutes evidence of some weight, great or small, against all such authorities.

and late. The President did what he could by means of persuasion to prevent any reduction of wage rates, but whether his requests had any influence it is impossible to say; and if they did, it is problematical whether that influence was beneficial, harmful, or neutral. The Hawley-Smoot Tariff Act of 1930 probably had little influence on employment, but what it did have must have been in the wrong direction. The general resort by the state governments to sales taxes was probably second in adverse effects only to the restrictive measures put into effect by the national government in 1933 and later.

From April to July, 1932, the Reserve banks purchased approximately one billion dollars worth of government securities in the open market; but this action came two and a half years after the beginning of the depression, and after the index of the price level had declined from 95 to 66 and that of industrial production from 121 to 68. More than a year later, in the latter part of 1933, the Reserve banks purchased some four hundred million dollars worth of governments.

However, it may reasonably be asked why the depression should have reached greater depths than on former occasions on which there had been equal absence of preventive measures. The psychological, political, and economic forces that are responsible for a given depression's reaching the precise proportions that it does are too diverse to make complete isolation or appraisal possible; but in all probability it was the chaotic international conditions that were responsible for the unusual severity of the depression down to 1933. London was placed in a precarious position by the freezing of a large amount of its funds in Germany and Austria, and this fact had repercussions throughout the industrial nations. The effect on business expectations was adverse and pronounced.

After such striking failure to take remedial action on the part of everybody who had any power to do so, it should occasion no surprise that employment sank to low levels.

Surely there was a lack of investment opportunities, but for completely different reasons than those advanced by the stagnation theorists.

Nevertheless, if prompt action had been taken by the American government and by the Reserve System after the stock-market crash to inject additional money into circulation, output in the United States need never have reached so low a level as in fact it did, nor need the depression have been so prolonged; and substantial stabilization in the United States would have been a major factor in sustaining activity in other countries. Moreover, with improvement in internal conditions, international problems would have been much less serious. However, the absence of an announced policy of monetary stabilization would have made the maintenance of the price level and of output somewhat more difficult than would have been the case had such a policy been in effect in 1929.

I readily concede that the foregoing facts do not conclusively refute the stagnation thesis, but they place a heavy burden of proof upon those who hold that investment opportunities are now more narrowly restricted than during the 1920's; or rather, that they would be unduly restricted under a policy of monetary stabilization and conditions of competition no more effective than those that prevailed prior to 1929. In fact, the stagnation theorists have largely ignored these considerations.

Let us assume that price and wage rigidity have been reduced to tolerable limits, that the legislature has created a monetary agency which has been directed to act exclusively for the purpose of stabilizing an index of the (some) price level, that open-market powers have been given to this agency, and that the legislature has indicated its intention of promptly supporting the agency by fiscal legislation if this should become necessary. Let us assume next that the volume of private investment has slackened, the price level has begun to fall, and employment is declining. Under these circumstances the monetary agency will be required to purchase securities in the open market. If these operations are not sufficient to maintain the price level, the legislature will provide for an injection of money by means of a budget deficit.[6] What do the stagnation theorists believe would be the consequence of such action? Can it be doubted that the public would prefer to use a sufficient amount of their newly found cash to maintain the aggregate demand for commodities and services, rather than to raise progressively and without limit their propensity to hoard? Suppose that investment were not restored to its previous level. How could the increase in disposable incomes arising from the budget deficit fail to raise the demand for consumers' goods sufficiently to support employment at the optimum level?

If businessmen stubbornly refused to increase their investments, this would be a simple way to do that which Keynes and his followers contend is highly desirable, namely, to increase the propensity to consume. It is preposterous to suppose that the public would continue to prefer cash to goods, regardless of the amount of cash held. Those who desired to save and hoard could do so to any extent their miserly desires might dictate, since an offsetting amount of cash would be flowing continuously into the pockets of those who would find satisfaction in the purchase of additional consumers' goods. Savers could hoard, but spenders would reap a benefit therefrom in increased consumption. There would thus be not only an increase in the propensity to consume on the part of the community as a whole, but a redistribution of real income in favor of the spenders, who are generally the receivers of the lower incomes. It would be an idyllic world in which past investment had been so great that we were compelled by monetary means to sustain consumption at such a level that virtually all our resources were devoted to the production of consumers' goods.

[6] The manner in which open-market operations and governmental surpluses and deficits may be expected to operate will be examined in greater detail in Chap. 9.

However, it is fantastic to suppose that cash in any amounts would be preferred to investment at any levels of interest rates, short of zero, that might prevail. In reality there are vast areas still available for private investment if only we will provide the necessary conditions of stability. A wealthy community is in no such dilemma as Keynes would have had us believe.

It may be asserted that the quantity of money could not be continuously increased without untoward consequences, as indeed it could not be; and precisely because the position of the stagnationists is untenable. Inflation would surely develop before long. This would be the evidence that continued injections of money were not required to maintain employment—that private investment was ample to absorb the amount saved under conditions of full employment.

There is not sufficient evidence to suggest that any of the industrial nations have as yet made even a near approach to the conditions assumed by the stagnation theorists. However, even though such conditions should arise, no direct support of investment by means of public expenditures would be required. There need be no more than some minimum of frictional unemployment even in a wealthy community that is stable in population, in which there is no advance in technology, in which the propensity to save is high, in which there is no public investment, and in which the marginal productivity of capital has been reduced by the accumulation of equipment to so low a level that the resulting rate of interest will not induce savers to invest such an amount of savings as would result from full employment. Such a community should welcome, rather than deplore, a high propensity to hoard on the part of the wealthy; but it should not then fail to adopt the proper monetary-fiscal measures.

V

While variations in the propensity to hoard and inappropriate changes in the stock of money will have temporary effects on employment, the absolute level of liquidity preference or of the quantity of money has no influence whatever in determining the level of employment. To be sure, a high propensity to hoard, associated with rigid wage rates in the downward direction and a wholly indefensible monetary policy, could result in a continuing volume of unemployment much in excess of the unavoidable minimum. It is a strange conclusion, however, which imputes the whole difficulty to the level of the propensity to hoard when the problem could be solved by a reasonable monetary policy.

APPENDIX TO CHAPTER 3

Some Aspects of the Theories of J. M. Keynes

The theory of interest presented in J. M. Keynes's *General Theory of Employment, Interest and Money* does not make the rate of interest *immediately* dependent upon the aggregate quantity of money, however measured, and the liquidity preferences of the community as a whole. Rather, it is determined by the quantity of money available to the speculators and their liquidity preferences; and the quantity of money available to satisfy their demands is the residual amount after the transactions motive has been satisfied. The amount demanded for transactions purposes is itself dependent upon the level of income. The quantity of money is measured in wage units.

It may be of some interest, although in the end we shall discover it not to be very enlightening, to see whether this theory appears to be consistent with the actual behavior of rates during some specific period of time. In the following rough attempt to compare the theory with historical facts, I have used monthly figures for June, 1929, and December, 1933, where they can be had; in other cases I have used annual figures for the years 1929 and 1933.

Income in 1933 was 34 per cent less than in 1929, measured in prices of 1929, or 52 per cent less, measured in current prices for each year.[1] The total of deposits (demand and time) plus currency declined from June, 1929, to December, 1933, from $58,598 million to $44,310 million. If the latter figure is inflated by an index (1929 = 100) of hourly wage rates given by the Department of Labor for 90 industries, the result is $55,112 million.[2] These figures

[1] Simon Kuznets, *National Income and Its Composition, 1919–1938* (1941), p. 147.

[2] U.S. Department of Commerce, *Survey of Current Business* (1942), Supplement, p. 55.

for wage rates may not be so reliable as one could wish, but they are the best we have, and in any case a rather wide margin of error would not seriously affect the results for present purposes. This inflation gives a decrease in the quantity of money of about 6 per cent, whereas if the wholesale price index of the Bureau of Labor Statistics were used, the result would be an increase of about 1.7 per cent. If there were such a thing as a correct figure, it would undoubtedly lie between these two extremes. The large decline in income coupled with the substantial stability in the quantity of money (in wage units) would, according to Keynes's analysis, release a proportionately very large amount of money to meet the demands for speculative balances, and thus would have an influence in the direction of reducing interest rates.

Any information about liquidity preferences must be got at by indirection and, for present purposes, is not highly reliable. The velocity of circulation of demand deposits (excluding interbank deposits) for 100 cities in the United States, excluding New York, was 45.8 per annum in June, 1929, and 27.2 in December, 1933, a decline of approximately 41 per cent.[3] These figures do not constitute a measure of liquidity preferences, but they do clearly indicate the direction of change and give some notion of its magnitude. However, there is reason to suppose that the increase in liquidity preferences of speculators was very much greater than these figures would suggest. The corresponding figures for New York City were 116.2 and 35.2, a decline of 70 per cent. If it is reasonable to suppose, and I think it is, that velocity in other than speculative transactions would decline in about the same ratio in New York City as elsewhere, and that speculative balances are relatively larger in New York than elsewhere, it follows that the velocity of these balances declined by much more than the 70 per cent decline in the

[3] From a mimeographed statement by the Federal Reserve Bank of New York.

velocity of all deposits in New York. These facts suggest—rather tentatively, to be sure—that there was a very great increase in the liquidity preferences of speculators, which would tend, according to Keynes, to raise the rate of interest. Whether this influence could be expected to offset, or more or less than offset, that of the increase in the quantity of money available to speculators cannot be determined.

In an article written after the publication of the *General Theory,* Keynes made an addition to his interest theory which he looked upon as important.[4] It is that "finance" must be provided in advance of actual investment or for any type of output that must be planned in advance. He asserted that, while he had previously allowed for an increase in the demand for money on account of any actual increase in activity, he would now add to this demand that for "finance" to take care of an *expected* increase. If possible, we should take this demand for finance into account in our very rough attempt at statistical verification, but there is no way of isolating this factor. Perhaps the figures of the F. W. Dodge Company for construction contracts awarded will be of some slight value in this connection, since construction contracts, because of the necessity of advance planning, will give rise to a greater demand for "finance" than other types of output. The index number for these contracts awarded fell from 144 in June, 1929, to 45 in December, 1933.[5] This decline would tend to reduce the rate of interest according to Keynes's analysis.

We must examine next the actual behavior of rates from June, 1929, to December, 1933. Table 3 gives the necessary information.

The rise in the yield on municipal bonds and on medium-grade corporate bonds cannot be accepted as an indication that rates rose, since the yields rose because of the poorer credit standing of the issuers. The real truth is that most of

[4] "The 'Ex-Ante' Theory of the Rate of Interest," *Economic Journal,* XLVII (1937), 663–669.

[5] *Annual Report of the Federal Reserve Board* (1933), pp. 240–241.

TABLE 3.* INTEREST RATES IN NEW YORK

Type of loan or bond	June, 1929, per cent	December, 1933, per cent
Treasury notes and certificates, 4–6 months	4.8	0.29
Prime 90-day bankers' acceptances.........	5.5	.63
Call loans, new.........................	7.83	.94
Prime commercial paper, 4–6 months.......	6.0	1.25–1.5
Prime 90-day commercial loans............	5.75–6.0	1.5 –3.5
30 corporate bonds, Aaa (Moody's)........	4.77	4.50
Treasury bonds..........................	3.69	3.53
High-grade municipal bonds (Standard Statistics)	4.26	4.89
30 corporate bonds, Baa (Moody's)........	5.94	7.75

* *Annual Report of the Federal Reserve Board* (1933), pp. 150, 234–235.

the corporations involved could not have borrowed had they tried. We may safely say, therefore, that the complex of rates declined from 1929 to 1933. However, if we desire to single out some one rate as an indicator of the trend of *the* rate, we can do so in a fairly satisfactory manner by a process of elimination.

Clearly we should rule out the rates on Treasury notes and certificates, bankers' acceptances, and call loans as indicators of the market rate of interest in which we are now interested. These rates one would expect to fall relatively to other rates because of the fact that these instruments are very good near-moneys. Treasury bonds should be ruled out, since we are interested in rates paid by business borrowers. This leaves only three rates, those on prime commercial paper, commercial loans, and the yield on high-grade corporate bonds. The last of these three should probably also be ruled out, since the yield on any long-term private security reflects in some measure, even though perhaps small, uncertainty about the future standing of the debtor. Moreover, this uncertainty will itself vary, and thus the rate will include a varying amount to cover the risk involved. Probably prime commercial paper answers too well the requirements of a really first-class near-money to make the rate on this paper acceptable. This leaves only the rate on prime commercial loans. Any short-term loan that is first class has in considerable degree the characteristics of a near-money, but these commercial loans are not available as investments to nonbankers, which means that they do not have the qualities of near-money in such excessive measure as the other types of short-term paper in the table. On the other hand, the fact that they are short-term means that the risk element is substantially eliminated. Moreover, these loans constitute a large proportion of all short-term credit outstanding. If we accept the movements of this rate as the appropriate criterion by which to test the theory of Lord Keynes, we may say that, rough though our results are, they tend to be as consistent with his theory as with an analysis that makes the marginal productivity of capital the primary determinant of the rate. Liquidity preferences of speculators apparently rose sharply, but both the transactions and the finance demands declined markedly. Meanwhile the stock of money, in real terms, was substantially constant. Hence it is reasonable to conclude that the rate of interest, according to the liquidity-preference theory, should have gone down.

The above result should not surprise us. Indeed, it should have been predicted if our data were at all adequate for our purpose. Even though Keynes made the liquidity-preferences of the speculators and the quantity of money available to them the immediate determinants of the rate, he nevertheless gave a great deal of weight to marginal productivity, as D. H. Robertson and Jacob Viner have noted, when he allowed for the transactions demand and the demand for finance.[6]

Let us examine the liquidity-preference theory of interest

[6] D. H. Robertson, *Essays in Monetary Theory* (1940), pp. 11–13; Jacob Viner, "Mr. Keynes on the Causes of Unemployment," *Quarterly Journal of Economics,* LI (1936–1937), 158–159.

in somewhat more detail. It will be desirable to consider the effect of a *change* in liquidity preferences under conditions of a high level of employment, since, if the theory is to be perfectly general, it must explain the rate of interest during conditions of equilibrium and "full" employment, as well as during depression.

Assume, then, that something happens to cause speculators to desire to hold less cash (in real terms) then currently they are holding at the going rate of interest. Furthermore, assume the quantity of money (in monetary terms) to be fixed, and provisionally that the change in liquidity preferences leads, at least temporarily, to a decline in the rate of interest, and a willingness of businessmen to make larger investments. Enterprisers will increase their borrowings; but since resources are already fully employed, the effect of offering more money for investment goods will be to raise their prices immediately, and almost as quickly the prices of the factors of production and of consumers' goods as well. This must be so unless businessmen increase their borrowings merely to hoard the borrowed funds, or unless the funds are continuously loaned to one borrower after another, never being offered for goods or services. But the rise in prices will decrease the quantity of money in real terms; and according to the liquidity-preference theory, the rate of interest will consequently return to its original level. It appears, therefore, that the quantity of money, when measured in real terms, is the dependent variable rather than the rate of interest. This is merely an old idea dressed up in new words—the demand for money has fallen and the aggregate value of the stock of money has correspondingly declined.

In lieu of a decline in liquidity preferences, we might have assumed an increase in the stock of money (in monetary terms). The consequences would have been essentially the same—a temporary decline in the rate of interest, a rise in prices until the quantity of money (in real terms) was the same as before the change (in monetary terms), and therefore a return of the rate to its original level. If changes in the level of liquidity preferences do not, at most, more than temporarily change the level of interest rates, we must look for some other factor as a determinant of the rate of interest. Similarly, if changes in the quantity of money in monetary terms merely set in motion forces which will operate to maintain constancy in the quantity of money in real terms, then these changes cannot permanently affect the rate of interest.

I have provisionally conceded that a decline in liquidity preferences or an increase in the quantity of money (in monetary terms) would reduce the rate of interest. This might or might not be so, even though the quantity of money (in real terms) which investors and speculators hold is a function of the rate. If the decline in liquidity preferences affected only investors and speculators, a temporary decline in the rate would be the normal expectation; and likewise if the additional money were handed in the first instance to this same group. But, in practice, speculators are not likely to be the only ones initially affected, and if they are not, there may be no decline in the rate at any time. On the contrary, the rising price level would almost certainly lead to a temporary *rise* in the rate, if not immediately then at least very soon.

If the volume of bank reserves is changed, while the quantity of money (hand-to-hand currency plus deposits) outside the banks is not simultaneously changed, it is highly probable that the rate of interest will be affected, although again only temporarily. However, it is questionable whether a change merely in bank reserves should be interpreted as a change in the quantity of money.

There would be justification for placing any emphasis upon the speculative demand for cash only if this demand were large relative to the total demand. In that case there would be somewhat more likelihood that the initial, but still temporary, effect of changes in liquidity preferences and in the quantity of money would be on the rate; and regardless of the effect on the rate, the variations in the speculative demand for money would then have a marked tendency to produce variations in the general level of prices, granted the absence of a policy of monetary stability. In fact, I question whether the speculative demand for cash is of a higher order of magnitude for the whole economy than the movements of cash into and out of the balances of business concerns on account of seasonal and sometimes random fluctuations. However, regardless of the relative level of the speculative demand for money, and even though the amount of this demand is a function of the rate, there will be at most only a temporary effect on the rate as liquidity preferences and the quantity of money change.

Keynes's interest theory is not a theory of interest at all. It does not explain the *level* of rates at *any* given time. At best it merely explains *temporary changes* in rates. It may explain why the rate rises temporarily from 4 to 5 per cent, but it does not explain why the initial rate was 4 per cent.

On page 303 of the *General Theory* there is an excellent statement, with which I agree without qualification, to the effect that up to some critical level of output, an increase in the quantity of money (in monetary terms?) will result partly in increasing output and partly in raising the cost unit, *i.e.*, wage rates; but that beyond this critical point monetary expansion will increase the cost unit proportionately to the increase in effective demand. These latter conditions are designated as those of "true" or "absolute" inflation.[7] It is not entirely clear—to me, at any rate—whether it is intended to imply that under conditions of "true" inflation a further increase in the quantity of money will have no influence on the rate of interest. If this is the intended meaning, then clearly the liquidity-preference theory of interest, in so far as it is to be interpreted as a *general* theory, has been effectively scuttled by Keynes

[7] See also pp. 119, 301.

himself. If, however, it is implied that the rate of interest will be depressed, the admission is hardly less damaging to his position. In this case it would be necessary to conclude that there would be an increase in investment, but this could come only at the expense of consumption. We would then have a type of (forced) saving, which Keynes has himself rightly said would be a "very rare and a very unstable phenomenon." [8]

I readily concede that under conditions of less than full employment a decrease in liquidity preferences or an increase in the stock of money (in monetary terms) will increase the level of employment, and that such changes *may* temporarily reduce the rate of interest; but these effects do not make of the liquidity-preference explanation a general theory of interest. Infection will cause fever, but the normal temperature of the body is not maintained by bacteria.

The statement that an increase in the quantity of money, at a time of less than full employment, will lead both to an increase in employment and to a rise of prices is entirely consistent with the position of the classical economists and with that of those who have written in the classical tradition. The classical writers were usually concerned with the allocation of resources rather than the level of employment, and they tacitly assumed full employment for their purposes. This was a justifiable procedure, but it does not mean that they would have denied that an increase in the quantity of money (at a time of unemployment) would increase employment as well as raise prices, had they been confronted with this question. However, we need not depend altogether upon surmise as to their position on this question. Henry Thornton, in 1802, pointed out in an excellent statement the manner in which a *decline* in the quantity of money would lead to a decline in both prices and the level of employment, and there is no reason

[8] *General Theory,* p. 80.

to suppose that if he had been asked about the effect of an increase in the quantity of money at a time of low employment he would not have replied that both prices and employment would have increased. His statement merits quotation: [9]

> It is true, that if we could suppose the diminution of bank paper to produce permanently a diminution in the value of all articles whatsoever, and a diminution, as it would then be fair that it should do, in the rate of wages also, the encouragement to future manufactures would be the same, though there would be a loss on the stock in hand. The tendency, however, of a very great and sudden reduction of the accustomed number of bank notes, is to create an *unusual* and *temporary* distress, and a fall of price arising from that distress. But a fall arising from temporary distress, will be attended probably with no correspondent fall in the rate of wages; for the fall of price, and the distress, will be understood to be temporary, and the rate of wages, we know, is not so variable as the price of goods. There is reason, therefore, to fear that the unnatural and extraordinary low price arising from the sort of distress of which we now speak, would occasion much discouragement of the fabrication of manufactures.

Marshall likewise pointed out that a decline in the quantity of money would reduce the level of employment and output, and, while he emphasized the effect of a reduction, he also referred briefly to the effect of an increase. A somewhat lengthy quotation may be justified: [10]

[9] Henry Thornton, *An Enquiry into the Nature and Effects of the Paper Credit of Great Britain* (1802, reprint of 1939), pp. 118–119.

[10] Alfred Marshall, "Remedies for Fluctuations of General Prices," *Contemporary Review,* LI (January–June, 1887), 358. A similar statement is to be found in Alfred and Mary Paley Marshall, *The Economics of Industry* (2d ed., 1881), pp. 155–156; and this statement is quoted in *Official Papers by Alfred Marshall,* J. M. Keynes, ed., (1926), pp. 7–8 and the third paragraph from p. 9.

When afterwards credit is shaken and prices begin to fall, every one wants to get rid of commodities and get hold of money which is rapidly rising in value; this makes prices fall all the faster, and the further fall makes credit shrink even more, and thus for a long time prices fall because prices have fallen. At such a time employers cease their production because they fear that when they come to sell their finished product general prices will be even lower than when they buy their materials; and at such times it would often be well for both sides and for the community at large that the employees should take rather less real wages than in times of prosperity. But in fact since wages and salaries are reckoned in money which is rising in value, the employer pays higher real wages than usual at such a time unless he can get money wages reduced. This is a difficult task, partly because the employees, not altogether unreasonably, fear that when nominal wages are once let down they will not be easily raised. So they are inclined to stop work rather than accept a nominal reduction even though it would not be a real one. The employer, on his part, finds a stoppage his easiest course; at all events, by diminishing production he will help to improve the market for his own goods. He may not happen to remember that every stoppage of work in any one trade diminishes the demand for the work of others; and that if all trades tried to improve the market by stopping their work together, the only result would be that every one would have less of everything to consume. He may even think that there is a fear of general over-production, not because he is prepared to say that we could have too much of anything at once, but because he knows that when a long period of peace and invention has increased production in every trade, the volume of goods rises relatively to that of money, prices fall, and borrowers, that is, men of business, generally lose.

Thus the want of a proper standard of purchasing power is the chief cause of the survival of the monstrous fallacy that there can be too much produced of everything. The fluctuations in the value of what we use as our standard are ever either flurrying up business activity into unwholesome fever, or else closing factories and workshops by the thousands in businesses that have nothing radically wrong with them, but in which whoever buys raw material and hires labour is likely to sell when prices have further fallen.

. . . .

I agree with the general opinion that a steady upward tendency in general prices conduces a little more to the general well-being than does a tendency downward, because it keeps industry somewhat better employed.

Irving Fisher made statements to the same effect as those of Thornton and Marshall, although with a different emphasis and without reference to the rigidity of wage rates. I quote: [11]

The factors seeking mutual adjustment are money in circulation, deposits, their velocities, the Q's and the p's. These magnitudes must always be linked together by the equation $MV + M'V' = \Sigma pQ$. This represents the mechanism of exchange. But in order to conform to such a relation the displacement of any one part of the mechanism spreads its effects during the transition period over all parts. Since periods of transition are the rule and those of equilibrium the exception, the mechanism of exchange is almost always in a dynamic rather than a static condition.

To repeat, as to the effect of a change in the quantity of money on employment, there is no necessary difference between the classical writers and Keynes. Usually the classical writers were noncommittal on this question, but the few statements they did make in regard to it clearly suggest that they would have agreed that the effect would not be merely upon prices, but also upon the level of employment. Unquestionably they would have disagreed with Keynes, however, as to the manner in which a change in the quantity of money works its influence on the volume of employment.

[11] Irving Fisher, *The Purchasing Power of Money* (rev. ed., The Macmillan Company, 1926), p. 71.

If the liquidity-preference theory had been offered merely as an addition to interest theory which would explain temporary changes in the rate in consequence of changes in the stock of money or in liquidity preferences, it could have been accepted; but in fact it was presented as an independent and adequate explanation under all circumstances.[12]

One's reaction to the *General Theory* depends in part upon what one conceives to have been the intentions of its author. Was he merely attempting to explain fluctuations in employment? And was he interested, therefore, only in *variations* in liquidity preferences and the quantity of money? Or was it his intention to present a perfectly general theory, one which would explain employment at any time and presumably, therefore, even in a static state? If this was his purpose, he necessarily must have looked upon the absolute level of liquidity preferences and the quantity of money, rather than changes in these factors, as the essential elements in his analysis. To be sure, such changes would still be required to explain variations in employment, but they would play a minor role in the whole

[12] There are occasional statements which cause one to wonder how independent of existing theories Keynes believed his interest theory to be. Note the following: "We shall find that the mistake in the accepted theories of the rate of interest lies in their attempting to derive the rate of interest from the first of these two constituents of psychological time-preference to the neglect of the second; and it is this neglect which we must endeavor to repair" (*General Theory*, p. 166). The first "constituent of psychological time-preference" referred to is the matter of how much is to be saved; the second, the form in which command over future consumption is to be held. The use of the word "neglect" does not suggest that Keynes intended to offer a substitute for the received theories, but only to modify or add to them.

Note also the following statement: "The owner of capital can obtain interest because capital is scarce, just as the owner of land can obtain rent because land is scarce" (*General Theory*, p. 376). The clear implication of this statement is that marginal productivity is a determinant of the interest rate.

analysis. I raise these questions not so much because there is doubt about the answers to them, as because it is difficult to believe that Keynes should have meant some of the things that he explicitly said. While there are occasional statements that seem to suggest the possibility that he was interested only or primarily in fluctuations in employment, and while the tone of the discussion frequently suggests this point of view, nevertheless there seems to be little room for doubt that he was in fact attempting to develop a *general* theory. The following quotations serve both to substantiate this conclusion and to indicate the reasons why, at the same time, one might have some very minor misgivings about this interpretation.

> I have called this book the *General Theory of Employment, Interest and Money,* placing the emphasis on the prefix *general.* (*General Theory,* p. 3.)

> The economic system may find itself in stable equilibrium with N [the volume of employment] at a level below full employment. (P. 30.)

> Thus we can sometimes regard our ultimate independent variable as consisting of (1) the three fundamental psychological factors, namely, the psychological propensity to consume, the psychological attitude to liquidity and the psychological expectation of future yield from capital-assets, (2) the wage-unit as determined by the bargains reached between employers and employed, and (3) the quantity of money as determined by the action of the central bank; so that, if we take as given the factors specified above, these variables determine the national income (or dividend) and the quantity of employment. . . . Our present object is to discover what determines at any time the national income of a given economic system and (which is almost the same thing) the amount of its employment. (Pp. 246–247.)

> Since we claim to have shown in the preceding chapters what determines the volume of employment at any time, it follows, if we are right, that our theory must be capable of explaining the phenomena of the Trade Cycle. (P. 313.)

> Hume a little later had a foot and a half in the classical world. For Hume began the practice among economists of stressing the importance of the equilibrium position as compared with the ever-shifting transition towards it, though he was still enough of a mercantilist not to overlook the fact that it is in the transition that we actually have our being. (P. 343.)
>
> This that I offer is, therefore, a theory of why output and employment are so liable to fluctuation.[13]

The above quotations amply support the conclusion that Keynes, in fact, was presenting what he believed to be a general theory of employment. Indeed he made this point of view explicit so often that it may perhaps seem pointless to raise the question of interpretation at all. The fact that he also discussed the problem of fluctuations in employment is not in the least inconsistent with this purpose, since a general theory may explain conditions both of equilibrium, with or without full employment, and of disturbance. Nevertheless, one wonders somewhat at the statements that he is offering "a theory of why output and employment are so liable to fluctuation," and that "it is in the transition that we actually have our being." I emphasize this question of interpretation because I believe that variations in the quantity of means of payment and in the propensity to hoard cash are the bases of fluctuations in employment, whereas I am equally convinced that the absolute level of the volume of money and of liquidity preferences have at most a minor part in any general theory of employment.

It seems clear that Keynes did look upon the absolute level of liquidity preferences and the quantity of money, rather than fluctuations in these factors, as essential elements in his analysis. The consistent position of the *General Theory* is that conditions may be such that the system

[13] "The General Theory of Employment," *Quarterly Journal of Economics,* LI (Harvard University Press, 1936–1937), 221.

cannot become so adjusted to any level of liquidity preferences or quantity of money, regardless of what they may be, and stable though they may be and may have been for an indefinite period of time, in such manner as to make full employment possible. This supposed impossibility of adjustment rests upon two assumptions: (1) that wage rates are rigid, and that even though they were flexible employment could not be increased by means of a decrease in the rate of pay; and (2) that the rate of interest is determined by the level of liquidity preferences and the quantity of money. That it is the level of these last two factors, and not changes in them, that are the critical elements in the analysis is indicated by the following quotation, among others that might be given.

> [The rate of interest] is the "price" which equilibrates the desire to hold wealth in the form of cash with the available quantity of cash. (*General Theory,* p. 167.)

The partial approval of the doctrines of J. A. Hobson lends additional weight to this interpretation, since it was the contention of the latter that there is a prevailing tendency toward oversaving, not that the propensity to save fluctuates. Nevertheless, much of the discussion of change runs in such terms as to support the suspicion that Keynes was actually influenced very greatly, and perhaps unconsciously, by the important but transitory effects of changes in liquidity preferences and the quantity of money, quite dissociated from any considerations of the influence of the absolute level of these two factors under conditions of stability. He was writing at a time of an unprecedentedly low level of employment and during one of the worst periods of peacetime industrial disturbance in history. To have exaggerated the importance of these conditions for purposes of equilibrium theory, or to have carried over into a general theory considerations that might properly apply only to the explanations of fluctuations in employment, or to have ignored some of the factors that were responsible for the then prevailing conditions would not be surprising.

Speculation of this sort is perhaps bootless and rather uncharitable, as well, since it suggests that the author of the *General Theory* may not have been entirely clear in his own mind about what it was he was trying to do. To be sure, the difficulty may lie with my own "lack of emancipation from preconceived ideas." But until and unless that emancipation is achieved, I shall be compelled, like the politicians, to "view with alarm" both the theoretical propositions and the recommendations on public policy that were advanced by Keynes. In partial support of my dark suspicion that he was uncertain as to what he was trying to do, I offer the following additional quotations.

> In dealing with the speculative-motive it is, however, important to distinguish between the changes in the rate of interest which are due to changes in the supply of money available to satisfy the speculative-motive, without there having been any change in the liquidity function, and those which are primarily due to changes in expectation affecting the liquidity function itself. (*General Theory,* p. 197.)

> The relation of changes in M to Y and *r* depends, in the first instance, on the way in which changes in M come about. (P. 200.)

> He [Locke] was confused concerning the relation between these two proportions, and he overlooked altogether the possibility of *fluctuations* in liquidity-preference. (P. 343.)

The above quotations properly emphasize the importance of changes in the factors under consideration, but unfortunately this is not the usual position taken in the *General Theory.* It is somewhat like concluding that, since falling water will turn a water wheel, a body of still water will perform the same task.

Admittedly the classical writers—Ricardo, in particular—concentrated their attention upon the problem of general equilibrium, upon long-run factors. They frequently overlooked, or at any rate underemphasized, short-term considerations, the difficulties of the transition from one position of equilibrium to another, the fact that the economy, because of a continuous succession of disturbances, is constantly in a condition of disequilibrium of some degree. But Keynes and his followers have gone to the other extreme. Their "revolution" in theory consists, in part, of ignoring the very real problems that interested the classical writers, and, in part also, of presenting their own analyses, based on short-run considerations, as applicable under all conditions, and therefore as replacements for the classical doctrines of general equilibrium. They have deprived themselves of some of the most important guides in the discussion of problems of policy. It is not necessary to throw overboard classical theory in order that we may intelligently consider problems of monetary equilibrium, as opposed to the classical problem of general equilibrium. The two points of view are not in conflict; they do not give rise to a problem of "integration." They simply require a consideration of different aspects of the economy. To concern ourselves with short-run problems only is likely to lead to recommendations on questions of policy which would have consequences that we neither desire nor expect. To ignore long-run factors is pure opportunism.

That a change in either liquidity preferences or the quantity of money will bring about transitional changes in the level of employment there can be no doubt, and I have indicated earlier in this chapter the manner in which it would seem that such changes will work themselves out; but it does not follow that there cannot thereafter be equilibrium with "full" employment, once these factors become stabilized at some (any) new level.

Keynes was correct in asserting that the maintenance of aggregate demand is of paramount importance, and manifestly a rise in liquidity preferences will reduce aggregate demand and, consequently, employment; but it is necessary to part company with him in explaining the manner in which this reduction in employment comes about. His conclusion was that the decline in aggregate demand is the reflection of a decline in investment, which in turn is the result of a rise in the rate of interest (or of a decline in the marginal efficiency of capital); and that a further, secondary, decline in demand, this time for consumers' goods, results from the decline in income. Developments may follow this route, but it is by no means necessary that they do so. It is more likely that either wholly or in large part the increased liquidity preferences will reduce the aggregate demand directly.

Chapter 4

INTERNAL ADJUSTMENTS TO INTERNATIONAL DISTURBANCES

I

International disturbances require internal adjustments to restore equilibrium. While the essential nature of these adjustments is independent of both the kind of monetary system that obtains and the monetary policy that is pursued, the details of the process and the difficulties to which it will give rise will vary with the monetary arrangements that prevail. More particularly, the necessary adjustment is a shift of resources, in one direction or the other, between industries producing exclusively for the domestic market and those producing for export; and a concurrent shift in the pattern of consumption such that different relative amounts of purely domestic and of international goods will be consumed. The inducement to these adjustments is a change in the relative prices of domestic (including labor services) and of international goods. This change in relative prices can be brought about either by an international flow of an international money or by a change in the foreign exchange rates between countries on independent national monetary standards. The question arises, therefore, as to which is preferable, an international gold standard with fixed exchange rates, or a national standard with flexible exchange rates? To this question there can be no definitive answer, although there are numerous considerations that bear upon it. These must be examined before any attempt at an answer can be made. In this chapter I shall present a brief restatement of the adjustments required by an international disturbance, and in Chapters 5 and 7 I shall consider various other aspects of the problem.

II

A variety of international disturbances is possible, and the corresponding changes in the national economy will be more or less different according to the kind of disturbance assumed. However, for present purposes it is necessary only to show that the essential nature of the adjustments is independent of the monetary system, although the details will differ greatly under the different systems that may obtain. For this purpose I propose briefly to trace the outstanding developments that will lead to a new position of international equilibrium after there has been an increase in the demand by one country for a product of outside countries, and yet more briefly to refer to the adjustments resulting from a reduction in the cost of production of an international good and from the imposition of an indemnity upon some given country.

In country *A*, which is relatively small, the following types of commodities are consumed:

1. Domestic goods, that is, goods that are produced exclusively for the home market.
2. Export goods which are produced for both the home and the foreign market.
3. Import goods which are domestically produced, but in inadequate volume, so that part of annual consumption comes from imports. Call these import goods *a*.
4. Import goods that are not produced at all within the country. Call these import goods *b*.

Let us assume that there is an increase in the demand in country *A* for an import good that is not produced at all within the country. Call this commodity *X*. We shall assume that international payments grow exclusively out of commodity imports and exports, and we shall abstract, for the present only, from banking difficulties and any untoward effects that the adjustments may have on expectations and employment. However, it is both because there may in fact be adverse consequences for banking operations and employment, and because these difficulties may offer greater obstacles to the reestablishment of equilibrium under one monetary system than another, that the analysis of this chapter is required. In the end, therefore, it will be necessary to consider these possible difficulties.

We shall also assume that conditions of increasing costs prevail throughout industry. This may not be an entirely realistic assumption, and yet it is probably not seriously in error. In any case, however, it is not my purpose to attempt an exhaustive analysis of the process of maintaining international equilibrium under all conditions. It is merely to show (1) that the essential "real" adjustments are independent of the kind of monetary system that prevails, and (2) that such difficulties as arise can probably be managed more satisfactorily with one than with another monetary system.

First let us consider the nature of the adjustments when country *A* adheres to an international gold standard. There is a very remote possibility that the exchange rates would decline[1] in that country and gold flow in, but any such development would require that the total of imports decrease and that the consumption of domestic goods rise, at the same time that the prices of international goods were constant and those of domestic goods were rising. That these would be the consequences of a decline in the ex-

[1] I shall use the terms "high" and "low," when applied to the exchange rates of a given country, consistently (I hope) to mean a high or a low price of a foreign currency in terms of the domestic currency. Thus I shall refer to a given rate for English and American currencies as being high (or low) for the British, but as low (or high) for the United States.

change rates can readily be seen from the fact that such a decline would mean an inflow of gold and therefore a rise in the prices of domestic goods. Such a development is highly improbable. We may assume, therefore, that the volume of imports would increase, demand for foreign exchange would rise, and the exchange rate would rise to the gold-export point.

The supply of foreign exchange would be depleted and exchange dealers would export gold to provide additional supplies; domestic prices would decline, including wage rates; and therefore money income would also be reduced. There could be no significant effect upon the prices of international goods in country *A*, however, since any given international commodity must have the same price in all countries on an international standard, abstracting from transportation costs and import duties. To be sure, there might be an inconsequential and temporary *rise* in the prices of these goods in *A* as a result of the rise in the foreign exchange rates (to the gold-export point) in that country. For present purposes, however, we are justified in assuming no substantial changes in the prices of these goods. Consumption of all four groups of commodities, exclusive of commodity *X*, would almost certainly decline in country *A*. Consumption includes investment.

The decline in domestic prices would reduce costs of production, and therefore the cost-price relationships in the international-goods industries would be improved, while there would be no such improvement in the domestic-goods industries. These changes in cost-price relationships, and the shift in the pattern of demand consequent upon the change in relative prices and upon the increased demand for commodity *X* alike would operate to reallocate the productive resources of the country. Since the relative prices of export commodities would have risen (because of the decline in domestic prices), their consumption would decline; but the domestic production of these commodities for the export market would rise by more than an equivalent amount, the increase in production being induced by the improvement in the cost-price relationships of the international-goods industries.

Imports of other goods than commodity *X* would decline, but not by so much as the increase in imports of the latter. The decline in imports of these commodities could be greater than the increase in imports of commodity *X* only if, to repeat, the consumption of other import goods fell and that of domestic goods rose, at the same time that the prices of international goods were constant and those of domestic goods were rising. Consumption of the total of all import goods other than *X* would decline, but the domestic production of import goods *a* would increase. The increase in domestic production of the latter goods would necessarily be less than the decline in imports of these goods. Otherwise there would be no decline in their consumption.

The major effects of the assumed disturbance in country *A*, therefore, would be a decline in domestic prices, including wage rates, and a shift of manufacturing resources from the production of domestic to the production of international goods.

Next let us assume that all conditions are the same as in the preceding analysis, except that country *A* maintains an independent, national, monetary system and flexible foreign exchange rates. In this case we must stipulate the national monetary policy that is to be followed, since some policy must prevail, either deliberately or by default; and the consequences of the increased demand for commodity *X* will in some of their details depend upon this policy. It will be best, for the purpose of indicating most sharply the possible differences between this case and that of an international standard, if we assume that money income is stabilized in country *A* and in all other countries with which it has trading relations. That in practice this would be the most feasible policy to follow is doubtful, but that question will be considered in Chapter 7. In any case, however, the adjustments in our analysis that must be made for a different policy can be introduced without difficulty. The assumption of a stable national money income will mean (in the short run in which we are now interested) substantial stability in the level of wage rates, but it will not mean an equal degree of stability in the price level of domestic commodities, since we are assuming that conditions of increasing costs prevail.

As the volume of imports rose in consequence of the increased demand for commodity *X*, the demand for foreign exchange would rise and, therefore, the exchange rate. Since no currency could flow out in payment for the imports there would be no predetermined level beyond which the exchange rate could not rise. However, as the exchange rate rose, the prices of international goods in country *A* would rise correspondingly. This must be so, since otherwise the prices of these goods would not be the same when converted into the currency of country *A* by way of the ruling exchange rates for that currency, in country *A* and in other countries.[2]

By assumption, monetary policy is such that money income is stable. Since we are assuming that conditions of increasing costs prevail, and since consumption of domestic goods will fall, the prices of domestic commodities will probably decline slightly, although there may be an opposing influence. If imported materials are used in the production of domestic goods, this fact will tend to raise their costs of

[2] The equivalence of prices for international goods, when converted from one currency into the other at ruling rates of exchange, could be maintained either by means of a rise of prices in *A*, by a fall of prices in other countries, or by some combination of these two developments. If *A* chanced to be the sole or primary source of supply for an international good, there might then be some downward adjustment of the price of that commodity in other countries, together with a smaller rise in its price in *A* than in the prices of other international goods and of foreign currencies. Except for this possibility, however, with our assumption that *A* is small, the adjustment will come at least preponderantly, and probably entirely, through a rise of prices in *A*.

production. But even so, the prices of domestic goods will probably decline somewhat, since the major portion of costs (most notably labor costs) must derive from the use of purely domestic materials and services. In any case, the prices of domestic commodities and wage rates will decline *relatively* to the prices of international goods, and therefore the cost-price relationships in the industries producing the latter goods will be improved.

The net effect is that the same shifts in resources and in consumption (including investment) are made under the national and the international standards. The *relative* prices of international goods rise under both standards, and in both cases the output of these goods increases while that of domestic goods declines. The direction of the changes in prices, consumption, production, imports, and exports is summarized in Table 4, and similarly the changes

TABLE 4. DIRECTION OF CHANGES IN THE READJUSTING PROCESS IN CASE OF AN OUTFLOW OF GOLD, OR OF A RISE IN EXCHANGE RATES UNDER A NATIONAL STANDARD *

Commodity	Price		Domestic production	Domestic consumption	Imports	Exports
	International standard	National standard				
Domestic goods	−	−	−	−	0	0
Labor	−	=				
Import goods a	=	+	+	−	−	0
Import goods b	=	+	0	−	−	0
Commodity X	=	+	0	+	+	0
All import goods ($a + b + X$)	=	+	+	+	+	0
Export goods	=	+	+	−	0	+

* Equality (=) indicates no change; plus (+), an increase; minus (−), a decrease; zero (0), no domestic production, imports, or exports, as the case may be.

in the unlikely case of an import of gold (or a decline in exchange rates under a national standard) are shown in Table 5.

TABLE 5. DIRECTION OF CHANGES IN THE READJUSTMENT PROCESS IN CASE OF AN INFLOW OF GOLD, OR OF A DECLINE IN EXCHANGE RATES UNDER A NATIONAL STANDARD *

Commodity	Price		Domestic production	Domestic consumption	Imports	Exports
	International standard	National standard				
Domestic goods....	+	+	+	+	0	0
Labor............	+	=				
Import goods *a*....	=	−	−	−, + } −	−, + } −	0
Import goods *b*....	=	−	0	−, + }	−, + }	0
Commodity *X*.....	=	−	0	+	+	0
All import goods ($a + b + X$)....	=	−	−	−	−	0
Export goods......	=	−	−	−	0	−

* Equality (=) indicates no change; plus (+), an increase; minus (−), a decrease; zero (0), no domestic production, imports, or exports, as the case may be.

In Table 4 the prices of domestic commodities decline under the international standard, both because of the decrease in the quantity of money and because of the assumed prevalence of increasing costs. Wage rates decline under this standard also, but not by so much, since their decline is due to the decrease in the quantity of money alone. Under the national standard the prices of domestic commodities decline only because output is assumed to be subject to increasing costs, and wage rates are constant because it is assumed that the aim of monetary policy is to stabilize money income. In Table 5 the prices of domestic goods under the international standard rise because of increasing costs and of the increase in the quantity of money, while wage rates rise only for the latter reason and, therefore, less than the prices of commodities. Under the national standard the prices of domestic goods rise because of increasing costs, and wage rates are constant in consequence of the established monetary policy.

Perhaps it is in order to consider further the statement that in the usual case, as depicted in Table 4, the consumption of domestic goods would decline, despite the fall in their relative prices. This fact can be most easily seen if we use for illustrative purposes the case of a national monetary system with fixed money income. Exchange rates may either go up, go down, or remain constant. If the increased consumption of commodity X were exclusively at the expense of other imports, manifestly there would be no change in the exchange rates, no change in prices, and no reallocation of resources in country A.

If the offset to the increased consumption of commodity X is a decline in both imports other than X and the consumption of domestic goods, and this is most likely, there will be a net rise in the *total* of imports, exchange rates will rise, and the relative prices of international goods will, therefore, also rise. Thus the cost-price relationships for the industries producing international goods will have improved. But the increase in imports will require a larger volume of exports. If there is to be this increase in exports, there must be some transference of resources to the export industries. These resources, however, cannot come from the industries producing import types of goods for the home market, since the cost-price relationships will have improved for these industries as well as for the export industries. In fact, because of this improvement there will be an increase in the output (but not in the consumption) of these import goods as well as of exports. On the other hand, the cost-price relationships of the domestic-goods industries will have been worsened, and they will therefore readily release resources. These resources are manifestly those that will permit the increase in exports. In the final analysis, imports of other import commodities than *X* will decline, and so also will consumption of domestic goods, but by a relatively smaller amount. Consumption of export goods will, of course, also decline.

If the public were to be successful in an attempt to increase their consumption of domestic goods, the prices of these goods would have to rise relatively to those of international goods, since only in this way could the necessary resources for an increased output of domestic goods be obtained. Such an increase in the relative prices of domestic goods would be possible only if exchange rates declined. But if exchange rates declined, we should have the unlikely case of a decrease in the consumption of international goods in the aggregate at the same time that their prices were falling and the demand for one of them (commodity *X*) was increasing. Perhaps Table 6, which is somewhat complicated, will be of assistance in bringing out the essential facts.

Money income is assumed to be constant at $12,000. In each of the three positions of equilibrium, the figures in the first lines of the first six columns give the amounts of consumption of each type of goods, and the sum of the amounts in the third lines of these columns gives the aggregate value of consumption (including investment). Column 7 gives the exports, and their value must be equal to the sum of the value of the imports as given in the third line of columns 3, 4, and 5. The total production of export goods is the sum of the amounts in columns 6 and 7. The total consumption of import goods *a* is the sum of columns 2 and 3. Thus, in the original position of equilibrium the total production of export goods is 410 units, and the total consumption of import goods *a* is 140 units.

Table 6 presents three possible positions of equilibrium—one before the increased demand for commodity *X* (I), and two afterward (II and III). The second position corresponds to the assumptions of Table 4, and the third to those

TABLE 6. CONSUMPTION, PRODUCTION, IMPORTS, AND EXPORTS IN COUNTRY *A*

	Domestic goods	Import goods *a*		Import goods *b*	Commodity *X*	Export goods	
		Domestic production	Imports			Domestic consumption	Exports
	(1)	(2)	(3)	(4)	(5)	(6)	(7)
I	11,000 at \$1.00 = \$11,000	60 at \$3.00 = \$180	80 at \$3.00 = \$240	60 at \$4.00 = \$240	48 at \$5.00 = \$240	50 at \$2.00 = \$100	360 at \$2.00 = \$720
II	10,982 at \$0.99 = \$10,872	70 at \$3.15 = \$220	66 at \$3.15 = \$208	58 at \$4.20 = \$244	68 at \$5.25 = \$357	47 at \$2.10 = \$99	385 at \$2.10 = \$809
III	11,019 at \$1.01 = \$11,129	56 at \$2.85 = \$160	50 at \$2.85 = \$143	55 at \$3.80 = \$209	60 at \$4.75 = \$285	39 at \$1.90 = \$74	335 at \$1.90 = \$637

of Table 5. In the second case the exchange rates are assumed to have risen by 5 per cent, in consequence of a net increase in imports and, therefore, the prices of all international goods to have risen by a corresponding percentage. Domestic goods, on the other hand, are assumed to have fallen in price by 1 per cent because of the prevailing conditions of increasing costs. The domestic production of export goods and of import goods *a* must rise, since their cost-price relationships have improved. The necessary rise in the production of export goods can take place only if consumption of domestic goods declines, since any decline in consumption of export goods must be offset by a rise in imports (and therefore exports) in order merely to avoid a *decline* in the output of export goods.

Table 7 depicts the changes that must take place in the process of restoring equilibrium. Lines III and IV are derived

TABLE 7. CHANGES IN PRODUCTION AND CONSUMPTION *

	Domestic goods; production and consumption (1)	Import goods *a*; production (2)	All imports (3)	Export goods: Consumption (4)	Export goods: Exports (5)
I	−129	+40	+89	=	+89
II	−130	+40	+89	+1	+89
III	−128	+40	+89	−1	+89
IV	+129	−20	−83	−26	−83

* Equality (=) indicates no change; plus (+), an increase; minus (−), a decrease. Quantities are in value terms.

from cases II and III, respectively, of Table 6, and lines I and II are further possibilities that are included for illustrative purposes. Changes in consumption are reflected in the first four columns, and their sum, therefore, must be zero in each case. The figures in columns 3 and 5 must be equal.

If we assume that the consumption of import goods, other than commodity *X*, does decrease sufficiently to permit an increase in the amount of domestic goods consumed, it means that total imports must decline, and the exchange rates and the prices of international goods must therefore fall. Then we have the situation reflected in Table 5, the third set of figures in Table 6, and the fourth line of Table 7, in which the consumption of import goods other than commodity *X* falls, in spite of the fact that their prices have declined. It is only under these improbable circumstances that the consumption of domestic goods may rise.

In countries that exported commodity *X* the adjustments would be substantially the reverse of those in country *A*, except that the output of commodity *X* would rise, whereas the output of other exportable commodities would tend to fall. However, the extent of the adjustments in the country or countries of supply might be far less than in country *A* and might, indeed, be so slight as to be of little consequence. This might be so, even though the production of commodity *X* were localized in some other small country. The assumption that country *A* is small means that the demand of this country for commodity *X* constitutes only a small portion of the total world demand, and consequently the increase in demand in this country would cause only a small rise in the price of commodity *X* in the country of supply and, likewise, only a minor shift of resources into the *X* industry. Only by an assumption that the demand and supply were each localized in a single country, and that the supplying country was not greatly larger than country *A*, could a large measure of the adjustment be thrown upon the country of supply. But even in these circumstances the extent of the adjustment in the supplying country would be less than in *A*. To be sure, there would then be a considerable shift of resources into the production of commodity *X*, but the inflow of gold (under the international standard) would raise domestic prices, and this development would, in turn, induce an increase of imports from third countries. Thus the supplying country would lose gold. Hence, while country *A* would be the sole final loser of gold, the gainers of gold would be widely distributed, and consequently the upward pressure on domestic prices in the latter countries (including the country of supply) would be much less than the downward influence in the former and might well be inconsequential.

Under the national standard and stable money income the exchange rate in the supplying country would fall, and consequently there might be some slight decline in the prices of international goods. However, this decline would be much less than the rise in country *A*, since, again, the change in demand in this country would be small in relation to the total world demand. Under both standards there would be a flow of resources into the *X* and domestic industries, but in neither case would there be any need for a general reduction of wage rates in the country of supply. Except in so far as there were obstacles to the mobility of resources, therefore, the required adjustments would not tend to cause unemployment in that country under either standard.

III

If, for other examples, instead of an increase in the demand for commodity *X* in country *A*, we assumed that the cost of production of this commodity decreased abroad, or that a continuing annual indemnity were levied upon *A* by some foreign power, the essential adjustments would be the same as in the preceding analysis. In the case of an outflow of gold under the international standard and of a rise of exchange rates under the national standard, there would be a shift of resources from domestic-goods to international-goods industries. In the case of a decrease in the cost of production of commodity *X*, however, there would be a greater probability of an inflow of gold into country *A* and other importing countries (or decline in the exchange rates under the national standard), since the price elasticity of demand for commodity *X* might be less than one. If this were true, payments on account of importations of commodity *X* would decline. Nevertheless, this would not necessarily mean an inflow of gold, since the difference between the former and the new level of expenditure on *X* might be spent entirely on other imports. Furthermore, the increased real incomes of the country of supply might induce larger imports from country *A*.

If the amount of the indemnity were greater than the aggregate imports of *A* prior to the beginning of payments on the indemnity, an outflow of gold (or a rise in the exchange rate under the national standard) would be unavoidable—the indemnity being fixed in gold under the international standard, or in terms of some currency other than that of country *A* under the national standard, but computed (for present purposes) in the latter currency at the rate of exchange ruling before payments on the indemnity began. This fact is evident, since the amount of foreign bills demanded in *A* would be larger than the preindemnity amount, and any increase in exports in consequence of the indemnity payment itself would be the result of a rise of the exchange rate and, therefore, could operate only to limit the rise, not to prevent it. Only if the amount of the indemnity were less than the preindemnity imports would an inflow of gold (or decline in the exchange rate under the national standard) be possible, but even then it would be highly improbable.

If the indemnity payments were greater than the preindemnity imports, any attempt of the public to maintain their consumption of domestic goods would simply cause gold to continue to flow out (or the exchange to rise under the national standard), since it would mean that there could be no increase in the resources available to the export industries. There could, therefore, be no expansion of exports with which to furnish the required amount of foreign bills for the payment of the indemnity. As gold flowed out, domestic prices and money income would continue to decline, but the amount of the taxes required to pay the indemnity would not. Therefore real income would decline drastically as long as the public persisted in their attempt to increase their consumption of domestic goods. Consequently, disposable incomes would fairly soon be reduced to a level that would induce the public to reduce their consumption of these goods.

If, under the national standard and indemnity payments larger than the preindemnity volume of imports, the public attempted to increase their consumption of domestic goods, the exchange rate would continue to rise, since there could be no increase in exports to furnish the necessary supply of foreign bills. The rise in the exchange rate would require a larger volume of domestic currency with which to purchase the bills required to pay the indemnity. Consequently, taxes would be raised progressively as long as this attempt on the part of the public continued, and eventually disposable incomes would be so reduced that the public would reduce their consumption of domestic goods.

If the amount of the indemnity payments were less than the preindemnity imports, the explanation of the improbability of an increase in consumption of domestic goods is similar to that given in regard to the possibility of an increase in such consumption in the case of an increase in the demand for commodity *X*.

The adjustments consequent upon a reduction in the cost of production of commodity *X* or upon the imposition of indemnity payments could, again, be illustrated by means of Table 6. The only changes required would be in column 5. In the case of a decrease in the cost of production of commodity *X*, the price in both the second and third positions of equilibrium would probably be down, but more in the third than in the second. However, if the demand of country *A* for commodity *X* were highly elastic, it is possible that the exchange rate would rise sufficiently to prevent any decline in the price of this commodity in *A*, although the price would necessarily decline relatively to the prices of other international goods. In the case of the indemnity, the annual amount of the payment would be substituted for the value of the imports of commodity *X* in column 5.

The preceding analysis reveals the nonessential character of the income effect in the maintenance of international equilibrium. If there is to be an effect of this kind, it is necessary that there be a change in real income, not merely in money income. If, for example, there is a decline only in money income, there will be no reason for a change in the pattern of demand unless relative prices have changed. If there is, in fact, a change in the pattern of demand, it must therefore be the consequence of relative price changes, not of the change in money income. In the case of the increased demand for commodity *X* there was no change in real income, although there was a change in the constituent elements of income. This would be true under either the international or the national standard, and consequently in neither case could an income effect be present. The necessary internal adjustment is that of a reallocation of resources. This is brought about by a change in the relative prices of domestic and international goods, which both induces a new pattern of consumption and changes the relative profitability of investment in the production of domestic and international goods.

In the case of the indemnity payment there would be an income effect, since real income after taxes would necessarily decline in country *A*. This effect would probably somewhat reduce the extent of the required change in the relative prices of domestic and international goods. There might also be an income effect in the case of the reduction in the cost of production of commodity *X*, since there would be some rise in real income in the country of supply.

IV

Up to this point no account has been taken of the operations of the banking system. Let us return, therefore, to the case of an increase in the demand for commodity *X* under the gold standard. Let us assume that at the time of the disturbance the banks are operating at their minimum reserve ratios. The export of gold would reduce reserve ratios below this minimum, and the banks would therefore find it necessary to contract their earning assets. Consequently, bank discount rates would rise in country *A*. But the influx of gold in other countries would tend to reduce discount rates in those countries. The resulting international differential in rates would tend to bring foreign loan funds into *A*, and this influx of funds would temporarily reduce the amount of gold outflow, thus making possible a smaller reduction of assets by the banks.

However, this could be only a transitory effect, since gradually the reserve position of the banks would become adjusted to the new conditions, at which time rates would decline to their old level in country *A* and correspondingly rise in other countries. Funds would then tend to be withdrawn from country *A*. These short-term international loans would, therefore, exercise no permanent influence on the situation—they would merely slow down the process of adjustment. Nevertheless, in so doing they might serve a very useful purpose.

V

Other instances of international disturbance might be given, but the examples presented are ample to indicate that the fundamental shifts in resources required in response to a disturbance are the same, regardless of the monetary system that prevails. The consequence is that there is no monetary means of insulating a country from the effects of foreign disturbances. The only way for a country to avoid these effects is to discontinue foreign trade altogether.

However, it does not follow that the adjustments required by a disturbance can be made as easily under the one monetary system as under the other. The same changes in relative prices are required in the two cases, but under the international standard this is achieved by a change in domestic prices, including wage rates, the exchange rates and international-goods prices being substantially stable; whereas under the national standard it is possible to pursue such a monetary policy as will not require an equal degree of change in wage rates. It would, indeed, be possible to avoid altogether the need for any change in wage rates, were it feasible to use an index of wages or of per capita money income as the guide to monetary policy. Unfortunately for other reasons such guides might not be the best for the purpose. The question of the most appropriate criterion for monetary policy will be considered in chapters 6 and 7.

It so happens that it is precisely domestic prices, but more particularly wage rates, that are most rigid; while, in the absence of exchange control, exchange rates and the prices of international goods are most flexible. Even though the price of an international good is stabilized by means of monopolistic control, it may still be flexible in terms of any currency except that of the country in which the commodity is produced. To be sure, under the gold standard, stabilization in one currency means stabilization in all gold currencies; but this will not be true under a national standard. Any international cartel that attempted to stabilize the price of its product in all countries maintaining independent national standards and flexible exchange rates would encounter grave difficulty. If, for example, the commodity were produced in country *B* and the price stabilized in terms of the currency of that country, and if in country *C*, which maintained a national currency and flexible exchange rates, the exchange on *B* rose, while the price of the commodity did not, it might be profitable (depending upon the cost of transportation) for dealers outside the cartel to purchase the commodity in *C* and ship it back to the country of its origin. To prevent such developments, the cartel would have either to raise the price equivalently with the exchange rate in *C* or to ration buyers in that country.

In view of the high degree of rigidity of wage rates, even in the absence of labor unions, the international standard clearly has marked disadvantages from the point of view of facilitation of any reallocation of resources within the economy that may be required by an international disturbance. In consequence of this rigidity, any disturbance that involves a loss of gold is very likely to bring on some greater or less amount of unemployment, and for the same reason the readjustment may be undesirably prolonged. Because of these facts, any nation that is losing gold is likely either to attempt to offset the loss of gold by an increase in its convertible paper currency or to resort to some device for preventing the loss of gold. In the former case the necessary adjustments are postponed, gold continues to flow out, and in the end the gold reserves are likely to become so depleted as to result in crisis. On the other hand, if some means of preventing the outflow is adopted, it will require measures that interfere with the gold standard to such an extent that the very real advantages of the system will be lost. Such interferences are of many possible kinds. Import duties may be raised or newly imposed, importers may be licensed, foreign exchange may be rationed, or a system of blocked currencies introduced.

The truth is that at a time of disturbance there is an irreconcilable conflict between the requirements for international equilibrium and for domestic stability. This conflict could be eliminated only if (1) we had a system of highly flexible prices, and (2) there were a high degree of mobility of resources. This dilemma has long been recognized, and many able writers have sought without success some way of escape from it. It is a matter to which Henry Thornton gave much attention in 1802; it was the crucial problem which gave rise to the currency-banking school controversy in England during the 1830's and early 1840's; it was a source of endless trouble for Great Britain during the 1920's; and it was one of the most important factors in determining the provisions of the International Monetary Fund.

Since there is no completely satisfactory solution to this problem, any policy that may be adopted will have some drawbacks. The question is further complicated, however, by the fact that there are numerous other and important considerations to which attention must be given before the most desirable policy can be decided upon. It is necessary, therefore, to examine these other matters before coming to any conclusion as to the relative over-all merits of an international and a national monetary standard. This will be done in the following four chapters.

Chapter 5

FIXED VERSUS FLEXIBLE EXCHANGE RATES

I

The presence of fractional-reserve banking has an important bearing on the relative desirability of national and international monetary standards. The banks are highly sensitive to withdrawals of reserve money. At the same time any change in the volume of their earning assets will affect the quantity of circulating medium and, consequently, the circumstances under which business enterprises must operate. An export of gold, which will require a reduction of the earning assets of the banks if they are already operating at the minimum level of reserves, *may* lead to much more adverse consequences than would an export of gold from a country in which fractional-reserve banking did not exist.

Whether an export of gold will in fact lead to a more drastic contraction of the stock of money where there is fractional-reserve banking than where there is not will depend on circumstances. Where the drain of gold is small in amount, or where, though large in the end, it takes place gradually, the percentage decline in the currency is likely to be no greater with than without fractional-reserve banking. However, the required reduction in the amount of the currency may be large, and at the same time circumstances may require that the gold be sent out of the country within a short period of time. In this case the multiple contraction of the currency by means of the reduction of the earning assets of the banks cannot have time to bring about the necessary adjustments in conditions so that the gold exported will not have to equal the required reduction in the volume of the currency. If this should be the case, the multiple contraction will lead to a percentage decline that will be greater than was required for the purpose of reestablishing equilibrium. In other words, the quantity of gold exported will be equal to the required reduction of the currency, instead of a percentage of the latter, the percentage being the reserve ratio of the banks.

Even though the drain of gold be small or gradual, the banks and the public may become alarmed at the loss of reserves; and if the banks, for this reason, or because of the rapid diminution of their reserves suggested as possible in the preceding paragraph, do become cautious and markedly restrict their earning assets, the force of deflation will be greater than necessary, and serious unemployment and reduction of output will be the consequences.

Banks would be equally sensitive to withdrawals of cash under a national monetary system, but for the government to replenish their reserves, by means of open market operations, because of an internal drain of reserve money would be both possible and consistent with the requirements of any reasonable monetary policy; and no external drain would be possible. The difficulties of maintaining fractional-reserve banking and an international currency concurrently are great, and the recurrent development of these difficulties constitutes an ever-returning invitation to exchange rationing, restriction of the privilege of exporting gold, an increase in import duties, or other devices, as a means of protecting the banking reserve.

II

Concerning the influence of flexible exchange rates on foreign trade there is little of a theoretical nature that can be said, and even that little is inconclusive. Furthermore, there is no reason to suppose that statistical evidence would be of much value. Historical periods of exchange instability have been the product of monetary disorder. At such times the internal disturbances may well have had a greater influence on the external trade of the country than the fluctuations in the foreign exchange rates; and there is no way of disentangling the influence of internal affairs from that of movements in the exchange rates. Data from such periods, therefore, are of little or no value as indicators of the influence of flexible exchanges under reasonably stable internal conditions. Moreover, even though there might be found periods of free exchanges associated with internal stability, it would still be impossible to isolate the influence of the former upon the volume of foreign trade.

If the foreign exchange rates may move freely, it is manifest that the payments by an importer or the receipts of an exporter, in his own currency, may differ from the amount that would have been paid or received had the exchanges been fixed. This being the case, the final prices of commodities entering into international trade will be sufficiently higher than under fixed exchanges to cover the risk incurred. For this reason the interregional division of labor will be less extensive. The important question, however, is whether this increase in price will be sufficient to operate as a serious deterrent to foreign trading activities.

If there is a well-organized market for forward exchange, in which the volume of operations is sufficient to permit hedging transactions in any desired amount and at any time, the traders themselves can avoid the exchange risk at a cost which will raise the price of the product only slightly. A national monetary standard would undoubtedly lead to the development of such speculative markets for the more important currencies, but it may be doubted whether adequate facilities for hedging operations in minor currencies would be provided. In the absence of such markets, the burden of the risk would be greater, but it is impossible to say by how much.

However, a well-organized market for speculation in foreign exchange would not merely afford opportunities for hedging. The speculation itself would tend to stabilize exchange rates in the sense that it would reduce the extent of short-run fluctuations, although probably not their frequency. I anticipate that this statement will be contested, since there seems to be a current tendency to believe that speculation will aggravate fluctuations in prices. Any such effect as this would constitute a nearly fatal objection to free exchanges, since it would mean that the prices of international goods and the relationship of these to the prices of domestic goods might be subjected to large fluctuations. These fluctuations would often be disequilibrating, and thus the exchanges themselves might become a frequent source of disturbance to the domestic economy. I submit, however, that this view of the effect of speculation is mistaken. Under the appropriate conditions, speculation serves a highly useful purpose, and the profit of the speculator is the reward for a bona fide service rendered. If a speculator has a disequilibrating influence, he will lose money and be eliminated from the market.

If monetary conditions are unstable, and such as to throw all the weight of expectations in one direction, speculation becomes rampant and feeds on itself. That is to say, purchases are made preponderantly in the expectation that in the short run prices will continue their movement in one direction, because of the nature of the prevailing monetary instability, and without regard to any basic norm. Indeed, under such circumstances the concept of a general level of prices, or of an exchange rate, to which a return is expected, vanishes. Prices therefore may go beyond the levels that retrospect shows to have been justified, and in a sense speculation may be said to have been responsible for the excesses; although in a more fundamental sense it is the monetary disorder that is the cause of the difficulty.

If conditions of monetary stability prevail, our conclusion with regard to the influence of speculation must be quite different from that suggested above. If there is a definite and announced policy of monetary stability, there can be no expectation that the price level or the foreign exchange rate can continue moving indefinitely in one direction. Rather, the further prices move from what is more or less definitely thought of as a normal level, the stronger will be the action of the speculators in preventing their continued movement away from that level. To come to any valid conclusions concerning the influence of speculation in any field, this distinction as to the general conditions under which speculation may be operating must be made.

Despite the foregoing possibilities of minimizing the costs of exchange fluctuations, it must be conceded that there would be such costs and that they would have some influence in the direction of reducing the volume of international trade. Though I would expect this influence to be inconsequential, the truth or falsity of this conclusion cannot be established without doubt.

III

Mere *fluctuations* in the exchange rates would have no significant influence upon the profitability of long-term foreign investments and, therefore, should have none on the volume of such lending. However, if there were a permanent change in the exchange rates, the position of either the borrower or the lender would be affected under certain circumstances. It is important, therefore, to consider the possibility and the effects of such changes.

If there is an increase of the stock of money in a country which maintains a national monetary system, and if all other things than the quantity of money and the level of prices are unchanged, then the foreign exchange rates in that country will rise commensurately with the rise in prices within the country, given no change in conditions in other countries. This is one situation in which computation of the rate according to the purchasing-power parity doctrine would correctly give the new rate. If the payments on an international loan are payable in the currency of the lender, he, of course, cannot suffer a loss in consequence of inflation in the borrower's country; but neither will the borrower, since his income, in this case, will rise substantially in the same ratio as the foreign exchange rate. If, however, the inflation takes place in the lender's country, the lender will lose and the borrower will gain. Manifestly we can generalize our statement as follows: If the payments on the loan are payable in the stable currency, whichever it may be, neither lender nor borrower can lose or gain from the inflation; whereas if the payments are to be made in the inflated currency, whichever it may be, the borrower will gain and the lender will lose.

However, the above conclusion may not help much in forecasting the possibility of loss to the lender, since it may be impossible to predict which currency, if either, will be inflated. Consequently there may be a very real danger of loss to the lender if inflation occurs; but so also is there if he makes a domestic loan. If he thinks, therefore, that the chances for inflation at home and abroad are the same, he will not believe that he is running a greater risk from a foreign than from a domestic loan; and if he believes there is less danger of inflation at home, he can protect himself to as great an extent in making the foreign loan as in making a domestic loan, merely by requiring that payments be in his own currency. Inasmuch as the borrower cannot lose from inflation, he should be willing to make the payments in either currency in so far as this factor is concerned.

Free exchanges may undergo permanent changes, despite stability in the price levels of the countries concerned. Herein lies the fallacy of the purchasing-power parity doctrine. As we saw in the preceding chapter, a rise in the demand of one country for the products of outside countries will normally raise the foreign exchange rate in that country, and this higher price for exchange will continue as long as the change in demand conditions is maintained or until some other disturbance of an opposite kind eliminates it. Such shifts in exchange rates as these are entirely unpredictable, and their influence on the position of international lenders and borrowers is different from that of shifts due to inflation.

Let us assume two countries which maintain trading relations with each other, but not with other nations. In each there is a national monetary system, and money income is stabilized. In country *A* there is an increase in the demand for the products of country *B*. This will cause a rise in the exchange rate in *A*. If there are loans outstanding by the citizens of *B* to those of *A*, the lenders will be unaffected by the change in the foreign exchange rate if payments are to be made in the currency of the lending country, while the borrowers will lose, since their incomes will not rise, as in the case of inflation, with the rise in the exchange rate. If payments are to be made in the currency of the borrowing country, the borrowers will neither gain nor lose, but the lenders will lose. Since such changes as these in foreign exchange rates are possible and unpredictable, either borrower or lender must incur a risk of loss from an international loan.

The fallacy in the purchasing-power parity doctrine lies in the assumption that the exchange rates are determined exclusively by the relative purchasing powers of two currencies, whereas, as we have seen, the exchange rate may permanently change, even though the relative purchasing powers are constant. However, we must not make the mistake of inferring that the extent of changes in the exchange rate between two national currencies is unlimited when the internal purchasing power of each is stabilized. In fact, the limits within which such changes can occur are sharply restricted, although they cannot be determined precisely or in advance.

The limiting factor is to be found in the relationship between domestic- and international-goods prices. As the exchange rate rises, money income being stabilized, international goods rise in price, but domestic goods either rise not so much or not at all. Consequently, as we saw in the preceding chapter, there is a shift of resources to the industries producing international goods; and the greater the rise in the exchange rate, the greater this shift in production. If the rise in the exchange rate is due to some fixed annual payments not under the control of the citizens of the country against which the exchanges are rising, as would be true in the case of an indemnity, the exchange rate will rise until a sufficient increase in the commodity balance of trade is obtained with which to make the annual payments. The extent of the rise will depend, therefore, upon the amount of the annual payments that it is politically possible to impose upon a nation, and upon cost conditions in the export industries.

If the rise in the exchange rate is due to some such factor as an increase in demand for foreign products, the population of the country against which the exchange is rising have it in their power to stop the rise. The more the rate rises, the greater will be the change in the relative prices of domestic and international goods, and the greater will be the decrease in the consumption of domestic goods at the same time that the relative prices of the latter are declining. Fairly soon the public will cease to be willing to decrease their consumption of domestic goods, and when this occurs the exchange rate will have reached its maximum. By how much these factors would limit the possible long-run changes in exchange rates is problematical. It is as impossible for the exchange rate to rise without limit, for other reasons than inflation, as for a country on the international gold standard to lose all its gold, since the possible extent of change in the relative prices of international and domestic goods is limited. The amount of this change required in response to a given disturbance will be the same under the two monetary standards.

If foreign investments take the form of equities, there will be no borrower to assume risks, and the "lender" will incur only such risks from inflation as would accompany a domestic investment of a similar kind. Inasmuch as the return to the investor will be, in the first instance, in terms of the currency of the "borrowing" country, he will incur the same degree of risk, from exchange fluctuations due to other causes than inflation, as he would had he made an outright loan, repayments on which were to be made in the currency of the borrower. That is to say, if the exchange rate rises in the "borrowing" country, for other reasons than inflation, the investor will lose, since there is no reason to suppose that the income of his enterprise will rise with the exchange rate; and if the rate rises in the "lending" country, the investor will gain.

It is clear that there is some danger of loss to foreign investors in consequence of changes in foreign exchange rates, even though domestic monetary stability prevails; although the possible losses are probably small. However, under the gold standard, losses are also possible, although they appear in a different form. If gold flows out of a country, domestic prices and incomes are reduced; and if it is the debtor country which loses gold, the debtor will find that he has to pay the same amount of gold, but that he has a lower income out of which to make the payments. He therefore loses just as surely as though his country had been on a national standard (in which case the exchange rate would have risen against him) and he had had to make payments in the currency of the lender.

It is doubtful that foreign long-term lenders give much, if any, consideration to the danger of loss from exchange fluctuations or from gold flows and changes in incomes under the gold standard. Losses on international, as on domestic, investments have been preponderantly due to failure of enterprises to develop the earning capacities that investors anticipated or to maintain those of the past, and to political instabilities which have given rise to irresponsibility of the state toward private property or to the contractual obligations of the government itself. Unless and until those states which desire to obtain foreign loans show a consistent and enduring willingness to respect their obligations to creditors, they can expect to pay a high price for such loans as they may succeed in obtaining. Some doubt about foreign governments in regard to this matter and a feeling that foreign enterprises are in any case more precarious than domestic ones are the major deterrents to private foreign lending; and any attempt to promote international private lending by means of monetary cooperation is largely wasted effort. It is the responsibility and stability of national governments that count, not the monetary systems under their control or their willingness to cooperate with other nations in monetary matters, except in so far as the latter is taken as an index of their reliability. Nevertheless, investors as a class appear to have short memories. To the extent that they do, nations can repudiate their foreign obligations and continue to borrow, with some delay, from abroad.

IV

Flexible exchanges do not have the same relationship to short- as to long-term lending. The former is largely speculative, if we interpret this word in a rather broad sense. Even though a short-term loan is made for the purpose of taking advantage of higher discount rates in the foreign than in the home market, a speculative element will often be present, since fluctuations of the exchange rates, even under the gold standard, may be sufficient to reduce (or increase) any gain from differentials in interest rates. Where such lending is the consequence of domestic monetary instability and constitutes an attempt to transfer assets into a stable currency, the speculative element predominates.

Under the gold standard, short-term loans provide a highly desirable element of elasticity in international monetary relations. They may either eliminate the need for gold drains in small amounts or induce gold inflows, and in both cases render it unnecessary to adjust the whole national economy to gold flows of the sort that do not reflect any fundamental maladjustment internationally. Occasions for such flows of gold arise frequently and, granted that other things are equal, it is best that the price system be not subjected to the strain of adjustment to them.

However, the gain from short-term international lending is not unalloyed. Short-term loans, whether domestic or international, may become a destabilizing factor. If doubts arise about the future, payment upon these loans is likely to be demanded. Any such development may cause difficulties for the debtors, and it will almost certainly give rise to further misgivings about business conditions in the immediate future. The suggestion of Henry Thornton, Thomas Tooke, and others, that the central bank should hold sufficiently large reserves to enable it to withstand minor drains of reserve money has much merit. It is difficult, to be sure—as the writers of the currency school pointed out—to distinguish "temporary" drains of gold from those that arise out of a condition of fundamental disequilibrium. However, no great harm would result from the assumption that all drains, in the absence of clear evidence to the contrary, were "temporary" until they had reached stipulated (relatively small) amounts and if, therefore, all drains were offset up to this point by the monetary agency. If sufficient reserves to permit this action were held, there would be little need for short-term international loans.

Whether or not we should discourage all short-term lending, such lending is clearly undesirable if it is not in response to differences in interest rates, but rather is due to fear of depreciation of the currency or to unsettled conditions in other directions. It will accentuate a condition of international disequilibrium. Manifestly, international short-term lending is desirable (if at all) only in so far as it obviates the necessity of adjustments under circumstances in which there is no essential disequilibrium. Such loans are clearly undesirable when they themselves promote maladjustments.

The gold standard operates nicely to facilitate the making of short-term loans of the kind which make possible the avoidance of unnecessary adjustments. As the exchange rates approach the gold-export point, interest rates in the money market are likely to rise. On the other hand, the nearer the exchange rate comes to the gold point, the greater is the protection to international lenders against loss from rate fluctuations, granting that they are assured the international standard will not be abandoned. If the exchange rate is at or near the export point in a given market, foreign lenders will be able to purchase the currency of this market when it is cheap and, at the same time, be assured that their own currency will be no dearer and may be cheaper, when they withdraw their funds. Their profit from the interest-rate differential is thus assured, and they have a reasonable prospect of a speculative gain from the change in the exchange rate.

Flexible exchange rates would not operate to prevent the making of equilibrating short-term loans if internal monetary stability were maintained. Exchange rates would fluctuate more widely than under the gold standard, and there would be no levels above or below which it was known that they could not go. Therefore the protection to the gain from interest-rate differences would be less, but the possibilities of speculative gain from fluctuations in the exchanges would be greater. Furthermore, short-term international differences in rates would be less likely to appear under the national than under the international standard, since an adverse foreign balance would require as much contraction of the currency in the country against which the balance was running only if it were following a policy of stabilizing the prices of international goods alone, and this would not be the most desirable policy. It seems probable, therefore, that foreign short-term loans under the two monetary systems would be markedly different in character. Under the international standard they would be primarily investments to take advantage of rate differentials; to a greater extent under the national standard, speculations on the movements of exchange rates.

Nevertheless, the influence of these loans in the two cases would be in the same direction. In both instances a rise in the exchange and money-market rates would induce foreign lenders to enter the market. No actual funds would flow, under the national standard, but money that would otherwise become temporarily inactive in the hands of exchange dealers would be made available to the loan market. Whereas in the case of the international standard the desirable effect is realized through the avoidance of gold flows (or inducing flows), thereby rendering price adjustments of domestic goods unnecessary, under the national standard it is realized through damping down the movements of the exchange rates and, consequently, of the prices of international goods.

Whether short-term loans would function as well to avoid unnecessary adjustments under a national as under an international standard depends, therefore, upon the effect of speculation upon the exchanges. The effect would undoubtedly be in the direction of stabilization of the exchanges if there were a policy of maintaining internal monetary stability, if the public were fully aware of this policy, and if it were implemented effectively. If these conditions were met, domestic speculators would sell (and foreign speculators buy) a currency against which the exchanges had risen by as much as was normally to be expected, and these operations would serve to reduce the extent, but not the frequency, of exchange fluctuations.

There is no point in attempting to determine whether disequilibrating short-term movements of funds would be more likely to occur under a national than under an international monetary system. Either such movements are evidence of pronounced internal instability or they are the consequence of fortuitous and temporary influences. In the one case they represent actual or imminent breakdown of the monetary system, whether it be national or international; in the other, they do no great harm, undesirable though they may be. When an international standard is abandoned, something must take its place; and since its successor is dissociated from gold and the worst of the excesses frequently come after the abandonment of gold, it is tempting to say that a national standard is less reliable than an international gold standard. The truth is, however, that a crisis which will destroy the stability of a national monetary system will do the same for an international gold standard.

Protection from monetary crises lies not in any particular monetary system, but in the willingness and ability of the government of the nation concerned to manage its affairs in such manner as to avoid a breakdown. Our choice between a national and an international standard should be based exclusively on the relative prospects of maintaining internal stability under each and of their anticipated relative performance under conditions that reasonably approach stability. A national crisis that leads to a flight from the currency is not a product of the particular monetary system that obtains, nor can the latter offer any protection against it, although on occasions the banking system has undoubtedly been a factor in creating such emergencies.

V

Automatic operation is a desirable characteristic of the gold standard. If fractional-reserve banking were eliminated, an international standard could operate completely without governmental "interference." It is well to emphasize this fact, since historically emergencies have frequently arisen, under the gold standard, which have seemed to demand monetary action by the government. These emergencies, however, should not be charged against the gold standard. They have been the product of the operations of the banks and of fiscal policies that were destructive of monetary stability.

Noninterference by the government in the operations of the monetary system is desirable, if by "interference" we mean discretionary and irresponsible governmental action. Nevertheless, we should not allow ourselves to be deceived by any superficial resemblance between the requirement that, in a competitive economy, the state avoid, as far as possible, direct participation in the economic activities of the economy, and the desirability of avoiding governmental "management" of the stock of money. The final responsibility of the legislature in monetary matters is unavoidable. A purely automatic system is to be preferred, if at all, only because and in so far as nondiscretionary management of the stock of money in accordance with definitely established rules may present difficulties. Control and management of the monetary system is not on the same plane as that of restrictive regulation of business activities or of direct governmental participation in economic affairs. It is rather for the purpose of providing certain essential conditions of definiteness in which business operations can be carried on with a minimum of uncertainty. It is more to be likened to legislative enactments which provide for the enforcement of contracts than to "interference" with business in the usual sense. If direct governmental management of the stock of money in accordance with an established rule can be had, the need for an automatic monetary system is eliminated.

If monetary management is to be wholly successful, it cannot be dissociated from the fiscal operations of the government, and it must be centralized. Unless, therefore, an international standard can be permitted to operate in a completely automatic manner, it represents an anomaly. If managed at all, it must be managed by national governments, each of which is the final authority over its own monetary affairs. A centralized authority is out of the question as long as there is no international organization which has the power of taxation.

VI

Nevertheless, a limited degree of success might be had with national management of an international monetary system. If management could be restricted by a definite rule to the offsetting of changes in velocity or temporary and fortuitous gold flows in small amounts, there would be no objection; but I see no rule of sufficient precision that could be formulated for this purpose. If national management is to go beyond these limits, if it is to attempt the stabilization of some index of monetary conditions, the merits of such management will depend in part upon the criterion which is adopted. If, for example, an index of the price level of domestic goods only were stabilized, the international equilibrating mechanism would be destroyed, since any adjustment in domestic-goods prices would be prevented by the monetary action taken to stabilize prices, and the stable exchange rates of the international standard would prevent an adjustment by means of a change in the prices of international goods. However, domestic stabilization of the price level of international goods might yield fairly satisfactory results.[1] Nevertheless, any degree of success would probably require that the currency of a country making such an attempt be backed by a gold reserve of either more or less than 100 per cent, since the output of gold is unlikely to be of the right amount to permit a stable price level and reserves of precisely 100 per cent. This requirement, however, would not necessitate the continuance of fractional-reserve banking. In lieu of a reserve ratio other than 100 per cent, the gold content of the currency might occasionally be changed, but if this were done unilaterally, as would be the case if one country were acting alone, it would constitute a disruptive influence in international economic relations.

[1] This question will be further examined in Chap. 7.

VII

It may be suggested that an international standard could be managed by some one outstanding money market, in such manner as the gold standard is frequently alleged to have been managed by London or, more specifically, by the Bank of England, prior to 1914. Despite the frequent statements claiming that London in effect managed the international monetary system on behalf of all the industrial nations, as if it were an established fact (it has even been asserted that the pre-1914 monetary system was a sterling standard), I see no sufficient evidence to support this point of view.

The directors of the Bank of England clearly were keenly aware of the vulnerable position of the Bank, and consequently they watched its reserves with hawklike concern. They did, apparently, manipulate their rate so as to do what they could to prevent a depletion of their reserves and also to prevent what they conceived to be an unnecessarily high reserve ratio. In this way they doubtless had some success in influencing the small and irregular gold flows that took place or might have taken place, although even this conclusion is more to be inferred than to be accepted as an established fact. There is no evidence of any other desirable effects of their attempts at management or, indeed, of their having attempted anything more.

The operations of the Bank of England are more to be regarded as consistent with an automatic international standard than as an attempt at management thereof. The directors desired to protect their reserves when gold was flowing out and so raised their discount rate. Thus in some measure they put into effect a deflationary pressure, which was precisely what was needed if the outflow was the consequence of a genuine disequilibrium, and in any event they may have induced foreign lenders to send funds temporarily to London. As gold flowed in, they decreased their rate so as to take advantage of their larger reserves and increase their earnings. This action, again, was consistent with the requirements of an international standard.

There was "management" by London in these ways, but that there was any direct attempt to maintain monetary stability, or any very great incidental success in this direction, I see no evidence. On the contrary, the Bank followed no clearly established policy of monetary stabilization at home, London suffered intermittent crises that were of domestic origin, and it was unable to protect itself in any great measure from the effects of foreign disturbances. If the Bank failed to influence conditions adversely, its "success" in this connection is to be measured by the extent to which it failed to follow policies which are now quite generally thought to be appropriate to a central bank. In the main the Bank conformed to the requirements of an automatic gold standard. If there was a greater degree of monetary stability during the nineteenth century than during the years following 1914, it is primarily to be attributed to the absence of any great crises comparable in magnitude with the two great wars and the disturbances of the interwar years and to the fact that there was no significant attempt at discretionary management of the currency by a central bank.

VIII

Nevertheless, a hybrid system that would have some of the characteristics both of a national system and of an international standard, managed by one country, is a possibility. If a group of nations agreed to maintain convertibility of their currencies into gold, and if then some one large nation among them deliberately managed its stock of money exclusively for the purpose of maintaining internal stability, completely ignoring the requirements of an automatic international standard, it is possible that a considerable degree of success might be had.

With this procedure it would be desirable that there be some redistribution of the world's stock of monetary gold, and that the gold content of each currency be so determined that all participating nations could begin with a high ratio of gold to nongold currency. A high ratio would be particularly important in the managing country. This nation would then stabilize its price level or adopt some other and equally simple and definite policy, while the other countries would stabilize their reserve ratios. The reserve ratio would be quite ignored in the managing country, where it would necessarily fluctuate, perhaps widely; except that, if it became necessary to reduce the ratio very greatly to maintain stability in the price level, it would be preferable, by international agreement, to reduce equally the gold content of all currencies. This latter action would not only provide for more units of currency from a given quantity of bullion, but it would also increase the output of the mines. It would, therefore, in effect, subsidize the gold-mining industry; but this would be only in addition to the subsidy which is inevitably granted to gold mining when gold is used in the monetary system.

Variations of reserve ratios are, of course, nothing new. Under the gold standard as it has been known, reserve ratios have constantly shifted; but these changes have been purely fortuitous and completely disruptive. They have not been deliberately determined or managed with reference to a national monetary policy. It is precisely because of fluctuations in reserve ratios and the consequently tenuous connection between the stocks of gold and of money that the gold standard has not operated as a genuinely automatic international monetary system should; although, because of fixed exchange rates, it could not function properly as a national standard. Historically the gold standard has been a nondescript system, one of the more important effects of which has been to support the illusion that "sound" monetary policies were followed by any nation that maintained convertibility of its currency into gold. It is not chimerical to suggest that the gold standard, *as we have known it in the past,* has been an obstacle to the development of a rational monetary policy. If gold were to function as a genuinely automatic international money, reserve ratios of each country should be substantially, although perhaps not rigidly, constant.

Such a system as that suggested above would sharply limit equilibrating shifts in the relative prices of domestic and international goods in the managing country if that country attempted to stabilize an index which included the prices of domestic goods. The burden of adjustment to international disturbances would then be thrown largely upon the other countries. However, if the index were based upon the prices of international goods, the adjustments would take place as much in the managing country as in the other countries. If the foreign trade of the managing country were large, as it should be, stable prices in that country, associated with fixed exchange rates and stable reserve ratios in the other countries, would result in a near approach to price-level stability in all countries. The inducement to the other countries to agree to this policy would be the promise of general stability and a high level of employment in the managing country, since this would be a matter of great importance to them. A major, even though incidental, consequence of this stability would be a great reduction of the incentives for the creation of trade barriers in all their multifarious forms. Given stability in a country dominant in the field of international trade, the world as a whole would benefit greatly from this system.

Nevertheless, this proposal is not very attractive. It would provide fixed exchange rates, which of themselves are probably to be desired; but the prices of domestic goods and services would be required to move, rather than those of international goods, in maintaining or reestablishing a position of international equilibrium. In view of the rigidity of wage rates, this requirement, in my judgment, much more than offsets any minor advantages of fixed exchange rates.

The fact that such nationalistic states as Nazi Germany and Fascist Italy either adopt outright national monetary systems or so interfere, by means of exchange rationing, blocked currencies, bilateral trade agreements, or other devices, with the operation of an international money as to render it essentially a national system constitutes no evidence to the effect that a national money promotes nationalism or that an international money operates against it.[2]

The matter of paramount importance in monetary policy is the maintenance of conditions of monetary stability. The relatively minor advantages of one system or another in promoting international trade and lending should not be weighed heavily in making a decision concerning the merits of a given monetary standard. If internal stability is achieved, international monetary affairs can be left largely to take care of themselves. If one system has clear advantages in maintaining stability, the resulting income greater than that possible under any alternative will more than compensate for any possible deterrent to foreign trade that this system may offer; with the consequence that, in the end, the volume of foreign trade itself will be greater than would have been the case under a monetary system that offered greater immediate inducements to trade.

The preceding discussion has leaned in the direction of a national monetary standard. This is because I believe

[2] "Of all forms of nationalism, monetary nationalism is the worst." [Lionel Robbins, *Economic Planning and International Order* (Macmillan & Co., Ltd., 1937), p. 290.] If Robbins by "monetary nationalism" means the use of monetary measures for the promotion of nationalistic interests, one may agree with him; but if he refers merely to a national monetary system, implying that it inevitably leads to such use, I can see no justification for his statement. An international system can be as readily debased to chauvinistic national purposes as can a national system.

that the important practical difficulties in the way of monetary management constitute more serious barriers to success with an international than with a national system. Under a reasonable approach to ideal conditions for the implementation of monetary policy there is little to choose between a national and an international standard. Ideal conditions require flexibility of prices and the absence of fractional-reserve banking.

If these conditions prevailed, a loss of specie under the gold standard would result in a prompt reduction in the prices of domestic goods, and this decline in prices would not give rise to a critical increase in the propensity to hoard. Moreover, there would be no danger of banking crises to reduce the circulating medium or to accentuate the propensity to hoard. In other words, equilibrium would be reestablished fairly promptly and without a significant intervening period of reduced output.

To be sure, we should be denied the privilege offsetting changes in velocity by means of variations in the quantity of money if we desired rigorously to adhere to an automatic standard. However, given the certainty that the quantity of money would be maintained, even though not increased, there would be much less reason than now for violent swings in expectations concerning the future of prices.

But to state the circumstances under which an international standard would operate satisfactorily is to reveal their absence in all industrial nations of today. However, conditions that now exist do not constitute equivalent barriers to the achievement of monetary stability under a national standard. Under the latter a change in the current foreign obligations would increase or decrease, as the case might be, the foreign exchange rates and therefore the prices of international goods. These prices tend to be much less rigid than the majority of domestic-goods prices, particularly so since wage rates are included in the latter, and consequently the necessary change in the relative prices of domestic and international goods would be obtained without great resistance. However, it would not necessarily be true that no change whatever would be required in the prices of domestic goods. If the monetary policy were that of stabilizing an index of the level of all prices—including those of both domestic and international goods—then some slight change in the prices of domestic, as well as of international, goods would be required.

Under a national standard, the reserve position of the banks would not be impaired by an increase in the amount of current foreign obligations, and therefore banking difficulties would be much less likely to be encountered. However, if for any reason bank reserves were reduced, it would be consistent with a rational policy to maintain or restore the reserve ratio of the banks by injecting additional money into circulation, and such action could be easily taken.

Moreover, a policy of monetary stabilization, definitely proclaimed by the legislature, along with ample provision for its implementation, would afford an even stronger basis for stability of expectations than would complete stability in the quantity of money. In view, therefore, of the partial rigidity of the economic system, a national standard would appear to present less prospect of disturbance, of either international or domestic origin, than the gold standard, and it would provide more nearly adequate means of opposing such disorders as might occur.

The worst of all possible systems is that which we now have. It cannot be surprising if the current combination of fractional-reserve banking, (limited) convertibility into gold, unlimited purchase of gold at a fixed price, discretionary management by numerous monetary authorities, and the resulting uncertainty with respect to the monetary policy that will prevail leads to frequent periods of unemployment and crisis. When this kind of system obtains, an approach to the reserve limits is likely to result in panicky fear which will make matters inordinately worse. Moreover, those in control of the monetary system at such times develop an extraordinary timidity. They turn in baffled desperation to the supposed need for maintaining convertibility or for supporting the price of government bonds, or to some other equally unimportant objective, as the most important single task before them.

One might raise the question as to whether, if a national standard seems to have advantages over an international one, it would not be still better further to disperse monetary authority and grant to each of the 48 states of the Union control of its own monetary system. This is not, however, a parallel case. The national government of the United States does have taxing power, whereas there is no comparable international agency. Furthermore, the individual states have no monetary powers by means of which they may interfere with the functioning of the national monetary system in a manner comparable with the action of national governments with respect to an international money. This statement is somewhat exaggerated, since the states do have the power of chartering banks; but even so, the national government can, if it will, do much to control the reserve position of the state banks. Resources are more mobile within the United States than they are internationally, and to some extent interregional movement of resources can be substituted for intraregional shifts and for price adjustments. Moreover, if there is a high degree of mobility of population within an area and a relatively large volume of interregional trade, the mere convenience of a common money is of considerable importance. Nevertheless, it must be conceded, I think, that if each of the 48 states controlled its own monetary system and maintained stability within its own jurisdiction, no significant difficulties would be encountered.

Chapter 6

THE GUIDE FOR MONETARY ACTION

I

The essential problem of monetary policy can be stated as that of "rules versus authorities."[1] Is there a need for some one, simple, definite, rule for monetary action which would serve to eliminate uncertainty in monetary matters from the calculations of businessmen? Or are unpredictable developments possible which would render a rule unduly restrictive? Must we rely upon the discretionary action of monetary authorities to meet differing requirements of changing circumstances? From a slightly different point of view the problem can be said to be that of rules versus weapons. Would monetary stability, in accordance with an announced rule of action, create the conditions in which a competitive economy would autonomously maintain equilibrium and a high average level of output? Or is the economy so unstable in any case that a monetary rule would be of little assistance in maintaining equilibrium? In formulating a monetary policy should it be our chief concern, therefore, to provide weapons to combat developed depressions or booms of some magnitude?

[1] See Henry C. Simons, "Rules versus Authorities in Monetary Policy," *Journal of Political Economy,* XLIV (1936), 1–30. Reprinted in Simons' *Economic Policy for a Free Society* (1948), pp. 160–183.

There is a basic difference of opinion between the defenders of discretionary management and those who ask for a single, simple rule for monetary policy. Would a competitive economy be unavoidably and inherently unstable to a high degree, even though all the essential rules for its functioning were provided? The proponents of discretion believe that it would be, whereas it is the thesis of this essay that such is not the case. That there would be minor fluctuations in output under conditions of monetary stability is probable, but there is little reason to suppose that the economy would be subject to great waves of depression and boom. Frictional unemployment could be high, but this problem must be attacked by other than monetary measures.

The proponents of discretionary authority have not presented a careful defense of their position. They content themselves with assertions that "effective limitation on excessive and unsound bank credit expansion under changing economic and banking conditions must be accomplished primarily by the exercise of discretionary authority rather than by automatic or mechanical laws." [2] In an otherwise excellent article on the means of checking postwar inflation, Jacob Viner concluded as follows: [3]

> What is the general moral to be drawn from the analysis here presented? It seems to be that, until better techniques are discovered, the problem of inflation and of deflation needs to be dealt with by improvisation, by *ad hoc* and prompt reactions to changes in circumstances as they occur rather than by fixed policies set long in advance in accordance with long-run forecasts.

In fact there is no such "moral" to be drawn from his article as Viner suggested. He was concerned with the then

[2] Woodlief Thomas and Ralph A. Young, in "Federal Reserve Policy" (1947), p. 89, pamphlet No. 8 in a series on *Postwar Economic Studies.*

[3] Jacob Viner, "Can We Check Inflation?" *Yale Review,* XXXVII (Yale University Press, 1948), 210.

current situation, and what he said has little bearing on the nature of long-run policy. Nevertheless, in this same article, he himself has furnished one of the most convincing criticisms of his own position. It runs as follows: [4]

> If the inflationary trend continues, and if Congress does not deal with it by other means, can we be sure that the Federal Reserve authorities will act in the manner here recommended? I am not so confident as perhaps I ought to be that they will act with promptness and vigor. Central bankers, including the American variety, have traditionally been practitioners of the "too little and too late," constantly prone to making a virtue out of excesses of moderation.

Viner is right in asserting that central bankers cannot be relied upon. Why, then, would he give them great power unaccompanied with a rule for its use? Perhaps he feels that labor unions will be responsible for unemployment, and that an established monetary policy will tie the hands of the monetary agency in dealing with the situation. If so, he implies that monetary action is appropriate as a means of dealing with the problem of monopoly. It is not; but perhaps he has other reasons. The defenders of discretion persistently assert that changing conditions will require different kinds of monetary action, but they do not tell us just how it is that a fixed rule will cause trouble. They do, however, contend that the monetary authority should follow numerous guides to action, and they frequently suggest for this purpose indexes of the price level, of production, and of employment. They sometimes assert that the extent of speculation should also be considered.

The level of production and of employment are not amenable to control by monetary measures, except in the sense that monetary stability will provide the conditions in which a high average level of output and employment will be maintained. If price rigidities are responsible for a high level of frictional unemployment, conditions could

[4] *Ibid.*, p. 207.

be improved by monetary means, if at all, only at the cost of serious inflation; and before the inflation had gone far it is quite likely that this itself would create so great a degree of uncertainty as to make the remedy worse than the disease. Monetary action is not appropriate as a remedial measure for the economic ills of specific areas, industries, or groups of consumers or producers. Indeed, it is not in nature a remedy at all. It is, or should be, action taken to implement an announced rule under which the public can carry on its business activities without fear of unpredictable decisions and actions by authorities possessed of discretionary powers.

II

To say that it should be the function of monetary policy to maintain monetary stability is not to provide a criterion for the immediate guidance of those in charge of the monetary system. For this purpose we need some definite, simple, and understandable indicator of the need for monetary action. It is also desirable that monetary policy be consistent with some long-run objective which has general support from the public. In the past, a balanced budget has served as such a criterion, since it is widely and unpremeditatively believed to represent sound fiscal practices. However, there has also been a widespread feeling that changes in the value of money are undesirable, despite the fact that no national legislature has been willing explicitly to adopt a policy of stabilizing the price level. The first of these attitudes has undoubtedly been greatly weakened by the events and discussions of the years since 1929. One is tempted to say that this is fortunate, since any monetary policy that is dissociated from gold, and that is designed to avoid a secular decline in prices, must in the long run and of necessity be implemented by a budget deficit. Even so, however, the case for balancing revenues and receipts, *after inclusion in the budget of the necessary deficit for monetary purposes,* is as valid as ever, and it may well be that the loss of faith in a balanced budget has gone much too far.

If it be true that a reasonable rule for monetary stability would largely eliminate the need for weapons to combat deflation or inflation, it follows that the choice of neither the rule itself nor the means of its implementation is of such paramount importance as would be the case if we must, in any case, anticipate a high degree of instability in output, employment, and the price level. We need merely some criterion of action which is of such a nature as to convince the public that monetary stability will be maintained. Nevertheless, we can hardly hope that a mere announcement of intention to follow a given rule will alone provide the needed stability. We must, therefore, accompany any policy which is adopted with what promises to be adequate means of implementation should occasion for action arise. Much of the discussion of this and the following two chapters will deal with the probable effectiveness of given rules or means of implementation, on the assumption that the economy is in fact highly susceptible to disturbances which will require offsetting by monetary means. This seems necessary, both to convince the public that the program will be at least fairly successful from the start, and to convince professional economists who are believers in instability that adequate measures have been provided to meet even their point of view. The discussion, therefore, will frequently consider the relative effectiveness of various indicators, or of different means of implementing the policy, in combatting deflation or inflation, even though I myself am convinced that these are secondary considerations.

There is no one guide to monetary stability that is theoretically "correct," and it may even be doubted that there is one that has manifest and important theoretical advantages over any alternative. That there "ought" to be some one policy that would result in neutrality of money toward employment and output seems, on first thought, plausible; but reflection indicates that the merits of any particular policy rest in large part upon practical, rather than purely theoretical, considerations. If all prices were highly and equally flexible, it would surely make little difference whether we permanently fixed the quantity of money at some given level, increased it at some constant rate, or stabilized an index of the general price level or of any one of numerous sectional price levels.

Among the more reasonable guides to monetary action, some would require only that a given quantity of money be maintained or that there be a constant rate of increase, without regard to variations in velocity; while others would require that changes in velocity be offset by counterchanges in the stock of money.

III

From some points of view a permanently unchanging quantity of money would be very desirable. It would be simple, definite, and understandable. In the absence of perverse action by the banks, it would be consistent with a balanced budget. In all these respects—and they are important—complete fixity in the quantity of money commands a very high rating.

Unfortunately an unchanging quantity of money would require that commodity prices have a continuously downward drift as long as the volume of transactions continued to grow. Moreover, a growing population would likewise require constantly declining wage rates. Until wage rates become much more flexible than they now are or have been in the past, any policy that requires a continuous reduction in rates of pay is merely inviting unemployment and, if labor unions retain their present strength, industrial warfare. Even in the absence of labor monopolies, it is doubtful that an undue amount of unemployment could be avoided in consequence of the necessity of wage reductions.

A policy of complete stabilization of the stock of money would eliminate the possibility of varying the quantity of money to offset changes in velocity; but this fact might not be so unfortunate as at first it may seen. It is problematical whether velocity would be more or less stable than it has been in the past. Fractional-reserve banking indirectly exercises two opposing influences on variations in velocity. On the one hand, the perverse changes in the stock of money, through the contraction and expansion of bank earning assets, operate to worsen or improve business conditions and thus to change the expectations of the public and magnify fluctuations in velocity. Opposed to this influence, however, is the fact that under fractional-reserve banking the possibility of borrowing from the banks and of repaying undesired loans means that to some extent fluctuations in bank loans take the place of variations in velocity. While this operation is a stabilizing influence on velocity, it is nevertheless as disruptive of business conditions as would be the larger variations in velocity that would occur in its absence; and precisely so, since the two changes are simply different manifestations of the same underlying attitudes.

If fractional-reserve banking were retained in conjunction with a policy of stabilizing the stock of money, the possibility of varying the volume of loans from the banks would remain with business firms; but the influence of their actions on the stock of money would be offset by governmental action. Whether, therefore, velocity would vary within wider limits than it has in the past would depend upon the actions of the recipients of the additional cash put into circulation by the government (or of relinquishers of cash withdrawn) and upon the extent to which greater stability in business conditions would stabilize velocity. If, for example, the recipients of additional cash failed to spend any part of it, the influence of this factor would be in the direction of a reduced velocity; but whether this would carry velocity to a lower level than has sometimes been reached in the past would depend upon the extent to which a reduced pessimism growing out of greater stability in business conditions tended to prevent velocity from reaching such levels.

If the banks were eliminated, those who would have expanded or contracted bank loans would in some measure hoard or dishoard cash instead. Again, whether this influence toward magnifying changes in velocity would be greater or less than the influence of greater stability in business conditions is uncertain, although I would expect it to be less. Nevertheless, even though greater changes in velocity did take place, with a constant stock of money greater stability in total expenditures would be possible, since the possibility of adverse indirect interaction between changes in the quantity of money and velocity would not be present.

In any event, with complete fixity in the stock of money there would be some variations in velocity. These variations would probably be magnified if business firms were short-term debtors in large amounts, as in fact they are in the aggregate. Near-moneys in the form of short-term credit will at all times—in both prosperity and depression—cause velocity to be higher than otherwise it would be, since such obligations will in some measure be substituted for cash in "cash" balances. However, the effect of near-moneys on *variations* in velocity will depend upon the kind of instruments, whether private or public. In so far as they consist of national governmental issues, it is reasonable to suppose that their influence on velocity will be stable, since these credit instruments cannot be less sound than money itself. If there is any fluctuation in the demand for short-term governmental obligations, it will probably be accompanied by shifts into and out of long-term governmental issues, or between governmental and private obligations, rather than shifts between the short-term obligations and money.

The effect of short-term business indebtedness, such as accounts and notes receivable, will probably be quite different. Of a sample of twenty-five American business firms, large and small, fifteen increased their cash holdings between the end of 1928 and the end of 1931. Eighteen decreased their accounts and notes receivable. This is much too small a sample to justify any generalization with respect to the proportion of firms that managed their cash and receivables in this manner; but it does afford a striking illustration of developments that would have disastrous consequences. To what extent the decrease in receivables was the consequence of pressure by creditors cannot be known, although in part the decrease is undoubtedly to be explained by this factor. Creditors may have demanded payment and then may either have hoarded the cash or paid off their own maturing obligations. In the first case a reduction of velocity is the direct consequence, and it is highly probable in the second. To the extent that there was an increase in cash hoarding, the deflationary influence must be added to that of the general reduction in the quantity of money outstanding. Those who released cash necessarily did so to the full extent of the increase in cash balances held by others, plus the total reduction in the stock of money.

IV

A policy which has been frequently suggested, and which would also eliminate the possibility of offsetting variations in velocity, is that of increasing the stock of money at a rate roughly equivalent to the rate of increase in the volume of transactions. This policy would substantially stabilize the price level, although it might not do so precisely. Any change, however, would be exceedingly slow. Like that of a fixed quantity of money, it would permit changes in velocity to affect the price level, and yet the results would not be so serious as those of the latter policy, inasmuch as the recurrent necessity of general wage reductions would not be present to act as disturbances. Booms, however, would be possible in so far as the growth of output is the consequence of technological advances.

While a policy of increasing the stock of money at a

constant rate would without much doubt be very satisfactory, and might in practice work out not much differently from one that required offsets to changes in velocity, it nevertheless seems desirable to adopt a policy of the second kind unless it has countervailing disadvantages of its own. This is in part because of the need of adopting a policy which from the outset will be most likely to convince the general public that monetary stability will in fact prevail. If it is felt that the government will "do something about it" when money is "not circulating," there is greater likelihood that confidence in the program will be induced and that, consequently, little or no compensatory action will in practice be required.

V

David Hume in 1752 noted that while prices are rising prosperity prevails, and he therefore concluded that the wisest policy would be to maintain a continually rising price level. However, he clearly doubted that such a policy was practicable. While this suggestion has never received widespread support among either economists or the general public, there nevertheless have been occasional writers, from Hume's day to the present, who have been intrigued by it. Although the preponderance of evidence is against such a policy, the fact that prosperity does accompany rising prices is a matter of importance and precludes our brushing aside the idea without first giving it careful consideration.

Because of unequal degrees of flexibility of prices, a rising price level tends to distort the price structure. This fact leads to undesirable redistributions of income, to allocations of resources which are not consistent with equilibrium, and to speculative activity which promotes further maladjustments. Nevertheless, these facts by themselves are not sufficient to condemn a policy of rising prices. If a major catastrophe from the collapse of a speculative boom could be avoided, as I am convinced it could be, if there were no alternative policy that would maintain output and employment at high levels, and were there no injustice to receivers of fixed incomes, the case for a rising price level would be a strong one. The fact is, however, that neither history nor theory provides any evidence that a stable price level will not maintain employment. It is not even necessary for this purpose that investment be maintained at any particular level. If the propensity to save under conditions of "full" employment were such that more would be saved than would be invested, a continuous injection of new money in sufficient volume to maintain the price level would operate to redistribute real income in favor of the spenders on consumption goods. Theoretically and practically, therefore, employment could be maintained exclusively through the production of consumption goods.

It should also be noted that as long as labor monopolies exist a rising price level not only invites labor disputes, it makes them inevitable. In a free labor market, wage rates would spontaneously rise with a rise in the price level, although possibly with some lag; but where wage rates are fixed by written contract, there is no way of raising them to the equilibrium level except by negotiation. A most certain way of bringing on industrial warfare in an extreme form is to encourage labor monopolies and then adopt a policy of constantly raising the price level. Because of the resulting work stoppages and of the uncertainties created by rising prices, it is highly probable that in fact the volume of output under conditions of rising prices would be less than with stable prices, despite the fact of a high level of employment and general prosperity.

VI

Belief in the desirability of a stable price level is of long standing. Nevertheless, until recent years strikingly few writers have believed that deliberate stabilization was possible, and it is probable that even today only a minority take this position. John Law, in his *Money and Trade Considered* (1705), pointed out that the value of silver fluctuated, and he contended that notes secured by land would lead to a stable price level. Despite the fact that his proposed remedy would undoubtedly have led to inflation rather than stability, he should be given credit for seeing the need for stabilization. Ricardo thought stability desirable, but he believed that adherence to the gold standard was the most that could be done to achieve it. In recent years, Irving Fisher has been the stoutest advocate of price-level stabilization. Henry Simons has been the most convincing, although he was more interested in the fundamental problem of monetary stability than in this particular criterion of stability.

Stability in the level of prices is clearly the one objective, susceptible of attainment by monetary measures, which is of the most immediate and direct concern to the business community. We should not unnecessarily add the risks of unpredictable and devastating waves of inflation and deflation to those of changing demand, of the development of substitute products, of technological advances by competitors, and of a host of other risks that businessmen are heir to. The primary importance of a fair degree of stability in the value of money is strikingly revealed by the fact that when we consider alternative measures we invariably examine the alternative from the standpoint of its probable effect on the price level. If it appears that it will result in a serious departure from stability, we reject it. This being the case, it seems evident that any other policy can be preferred, if at all, only because of some insurmountable difficulty in the implementation of a policy of price-level stabilization. That there are difficulties of implementation must be admitted, but it is doubtful that any alternative policy offers significant advantages, even on the score of implementation.

VII

It is probable that the most effective opponents of price-level stabilization during the last twenty years have been the officials of the Federal Reserve System. A number of these officials appeared before the House Committee on Banking and Currency in 1926 and 1928, giving testimony in opposition to the Strong Bill, which would have directed the Federal Reserve Board to stabilize the price level. In 1937 and 1939 the Board on three occasions officially and emphatically stated its opposition to legislation of this kind.

In a statement of August 2, 1937, the Board asserted that the broad objective of maximum output cannot "be achieved by attempting to maintain a fixed level of prices, and that, therefore, price stability should not be the sole or principal objective of monetary policy." The Board went on to say that there is no agreement on the index that would be most suitable for stabilization; that "unstable conditions may develop, as they did in the 1920's, while the price level remains stable;" that under certain conditions "changes in the price level would work toward maintenance of stability," as, for example, during a period of advancing technology; and that there are other factors than the stock of money, many of them nonmonetary, which affect prices and business activity, but which cannot be controlled by monetary means. These other influences, the Board asserted, may express themselves in changes in the "rate of use" of money, "as well as in a change in the supply itself." The Board concluded that monetary management is not "an exact science, since it involves forecasting and dealing with many uncertainties," that "it is essential in determining an objective to leave scope for judgment and discretion;" and that "economic stability rather than price stability should be the general objective of public policy." [5]

[5] *Federal Reserve Bulletin,* XXIII (1937), 827–828.

As part of a lengthier statement on March 13, 1939, the Board succinctly summarized its objections to stabilization of the price level: [6]

> Experience has shown, however, that (1) prices cannot be controlled by changes in the amount and cost of money; (2) the Board's control of the amount of money is not complete and cannot be made complete; (3) a steady average of prices does not necessarily result in lasting prosperity; and (4) a steady level of average prices is not nearly as important to the people as a fair relationship between the prices of the commodities which they produce and those which they must buy.

The Board's appeal to experience in support of its position was ill advised. We have not provided the proper machinery for stabilizing the price level, nor have we ever seriously attempted stabilization. It may well be true, as the Board asserts, that a central bank cannot alone prevent undue fluctuations in the level of prices, and yet this is far from an established fact. The unprecedented decline in output and prices during the early 1930's offers no evidence whatever concerning the effectiveness of the rate and open-market devices at the disposal of the Reserve System. While the System did promptly reduce its rediscount rates in the autumn of 1929, the continued reduction thereafter was exceedingly slow; and it failed to purchase in the open market on a significant scale until 1932, when the depression had already reached nearly the lowest level that was to be encountered. We have no empirical knowledge to suggest what the effect of more prompt and vigorous action might have been. Skepticism concerning the power of the Reserve System cannot be supported by the citation of experience.

Reference to the 1920's as a period during which the difficulties of the 1930's were in preparation is unconvincing. There was very little "wrong" with the years from

[6] *Ibid.*, XXV (1939), 255.

1925 to 1929, and that little could have been eliminated or compensated for by a policy of monetary stabilization. To be sure, there were numerous bank failures; there was speculation in the stock market and in real estate; this speculation was bound to cease sooner or later and, when it did, some readjustments might have become necessary. These developments might well have caused some decline in the level of output. Nevertheless, our real failure did not lie in a mismanagement of our affairs in these years. Our mistakes are to be found, granted the absence of an established monetary policy, in our failure to follow an enlightened policy in the months and years immediately following the autumn of 1929. Neither the Reserve System nor the Federal government made any significant effort to prevent a drastic decline in the quantity of money, to say nothing of a much-needed increase, from 1929 to 1932. This is where we blundered.

The Board was right in asserting that there is no agreement on the index to be stabilized. This, however, is not the question for first consideration. A number of possible indexes would be reasonably acceptable, although certainly some would be better than others. While it may not be ideal for the purpose, nevertheless the wholesale index of the Bureau of Labor Statistics as it is now constructed would be fairly satisfactory. This argument is not in any case directed at the merits of a policy of stabilization of the price level. However, the question of the index, which is the chief subject for the remainder of this chapter and for the following chapter, will be taken up shortly for further consideration.

The Board was not correct beyond doubt in its statement that under conditions of advancing technology a declining price level would "work toward" the maintenance of stability, although unquestionably it would be *consistent* with stability. This statement again reveals the failure of the Board fully to comprehend the position of those who defend stabilization of the price level. They admit that a falling price level under conditions of advancing technology would not lead to maladjustments; but they see no criterion of policy which could be stated in terms of a price index and which would require precisely the "right" rate of decline in commodity prices; and they assert that any stable-price-level boom is a matter of secondary importance if policy is directed toward the maintenance of monetary stability at all times.

The contention of the Board that nonmonetary are equally important with the monetary factors in controlling the price level, that these may be reflected in the "rate of use" of money, and that such factors may not be controllable by monetary means is not a valid basis for opposition to a policy of stabilization of the price level. The whole case for stabilization by means of variations in the stock of money rests upon the admission that there are other factors and upon the belief that it is changes in the quantity of money which are both directly attainable and effective in offsetting the untoward effects of these other influences. If anything is to be made of a criticism revolving around this question, it must be shown, not that there are other, directly uncontrollable, factors, but that their influence cannot be offset by monetary measures. The Board's contention is somewhat like saying that there is no point in increasing the power of an airplane engine with an increase in the weight to be lifted, since the weight itself and the wingspread are of equal importance with the motive power in determining whether the plane will get off the ground.

It is notably true, as the Board contended, that a "fair relationship between the prices of the commodities which they produce and those which they must buy" is important to business enterprises; but the fact that this "fair relationship" is important does not mean that a stable price level is either unimportant or inconsistent therewith. On the contrary, this is an argument for, not against, a stable price level, since it is precisely while the price level is changing that distortions in the price structure are most likely to develop.

The Board conceded that "violent changes in prices are harmful," but asserted that "that does not mean that lasting prosperity is assured when prices are steady." The Board cited no period during which prices were stable and unemployment at a high level. About all that was offered in support of their assertion was the claim, already commented on, that the prosperity of the 1920's, which was accompanied by "fairly steady prices," was not maintained, and that, in fact, it was during those years that our troubles of the 1930's were brewing. If the Board members are to establish their case against stabilization of the price level by reference to experience, they must show that the experiment has been tried and has failed. This they cannot do.

The conclusion of the Board that monetary management is not "an exact science, since it involves forecasting and dealing with many uncertainties," that there must be "scope for judgment and discretion," and that "economic stability rather than price stability should be the general objective of public policy" reveals a failure to realize either the limitations or the possibilities of monetary policy. Monetary "management" is not, indeed, an "exact science." It is a confused practice, arising from lack of understanding of the needs of a competitive society in monetary matters. It would be fortunate if forecasting of economic developments were possible; but since it is not, the need for making use of some such current datum as a price index is greater, not less. If "scope for judgment and discretion" is left to the monetary agency, one of the essential elements of a good monetary policy will be lacking. It is by means of a definite, unambiguous, nondiscretionary control of the stock of money that most can be done to stabilize business expectations. The Board tends to concern itself so much with the unpredictable future that it ignores the present. It should discontinue all forecasting.

Furthermore, one may suspect that those who ask for

discretionary management believe that monetary measures can be effective in restricted areas of the economy, that they are suitable as the means for a piecemeal attack on the problem of stability. Neither are they suitable for such a purpose, nor is such an attack suitable as a means of maintaining general stability. Furthermore, it is becoming increasingly evident that we are likely more often to need protection from incompetent discretionary management than reliance upon fallible human judgment. The Board is in a weak position to enter a plea for discretionary powers, since it had all the "scope for judgment" that could have been desired in the early 1930's; nevertheless, it failed in meeting its responsibilities. And the mistakes of the Board continue. Stabilization of the price of government bonds is as bad a policy as could be conceived, and yet since 1942 the Board has apparently followed this policy to the exclusion of all other considerations. About all that can be said in defense of the Board is that any other group of men clothed with discretionary monetary powers might have done as badly.

VIII

Until recent years the demand for a stable price level has been based largely upon the effect of changing prices on the debtor, creditor, and fixed-income classes. It has not been usual, until very recent years at any rate, to consider the effect of technological advances upon the relative positions of debtors and creditors. The one exception among earlier writers, as far as I am aware, was Samuel Bailey, who analyzed these effects very well in his *Money and Its Vicissitudes in Value* (1837).

Under conditions of stable per capita output it is manifest that stable prices leave debtors and creditors in the same relative positions at the end of the contract as they had anticipated at the beginning. If, however, the commodity price level were stabilized, and if technological advances were made during the life of the contract, the creditor would receive in repayment the same value in commodities that he had lent, but a smaller value in services, inasmuch as wage rates would have risen. The debtor, however, would find that his income had risen, and therefore the repayment of the loan would be less burdensome to him than would have been the case had prices been stable and per capita output constant. In this case, therefore, a stable (commodity) price level will have meant a loss to the creditor and a gain to the debtor. On the other hand, if money income had been stabilized, the creditor would have gained, while the debtor would have found the burden of repayment neither less nor greater than it would have been in the absence of the innovations. The latter would simply have failed to share the gains from technological progress. To be sure, he would have participated in these benefits as consumer, but not as debtor.

Under conditions of advancing technology the determination of the effects of a given price-level policy on debtors and creditors is not so simple a matter as it is when efficiency is unchanging. Nevertheless, the stabilization of any sectional price level or of the general price level will not work much, if any, hardship on any group in the community. In this connection, about the only question that arises is that of deciding how we desire the benefits of technological progress to be shared; and even this is an inconsequential matter as compared with that of providing one of the essential rules for the functioning of the economy. We may safely ignore the question of justice in deciding upon the price level to be stabilized and may confine ourselves rather to the question of what would constitute the best monetary rule, inasmuch as no policy that seems desirable from the latter point of view will be distinctly bad from the standpoint of justice. This is not to belittle the wholly tragic effects of sharply rising price levels on those with fixed incomes; but a truly inflationary policy would not be acceptable by any criterion.

IX

The stabilization of any important sectional price level, or of the general price level, would serve as a reasonable rule for monetary action. Under conditions of continuously increasing efficiency, stabilization of an index of wage rates would require a smaller annual increase in the stock of money than would the stabilization of any commodity index. Indeed, if population were stable, this policy would require either little or no secular increase in the stock of money, depending upon whether the proportion of income going to wage earners were constant. Nevertheless, there would be no disturbance of equilibrium by the monetary system. Commodity prices would fall and would be expected to fall only in so far as technological advances were made, and therefore aggregate demand would be maintained at all times. If for nonmonetary reasons aggregate demand fell, this fact would place a downward pressure on wage rates and would require, therefore, an addition to the stock of money sufficient to eliminate this pressure.

However, demand would be maintained in the presence of disturbances only if wage rates were sufficiently flexible to give the signal for monetary action. If rates were kept up by means of monopolistic control of the supply of labor or by other nonmonetary means, they would always be stable, regardless of monetary policy; consequently, aggregate demand might decline and unemployment might develop without the signal for an addition to the stock of money ever having been given. While, therefore, stabilization of an index of wage rates would be a reasonable policy if rates of pay were flexible, it appears doubtful that in practice wage rates would have the necessary degree of flexibility, even in the absence of labor monopolies.

Stabilization of the level of wage rates is in harmony with the concept of neutral money, since commodity prices would fall with technological progress, and consequently no stable-price-level boom would be possible. The difficulty with the concept of neutral money is that it seems to carry the implication that there is some one monetary policy which is theoretically "correct," whereas actually there is no such policy. If there is a group of prices which are in fact rigid and which cover a large number of services or commodities relative to the whole economy, a monetary policy which would have required, under equilibrium conditions, that an index of these prices remain at all times stable, *had the prices been flexible,* would manifestly be very effective in overcoming disturbances. It so happens that wage rates not only answer to this description but are also an important element in costs, and therefore a monetary policy consistent with their stability under conditions of advancing technology would prevent the development of conditions similar, in all other essential respects than that of price-level behavior, to bona fide inflationary booms. Substantially this is all there is to the concept of neutral money, and it is exclusively the outcome of the failure of all prices to be highly flexible, rather than any inherent theoretical characteristic of a competitive economy.

Despite the attractiveness of a monetary policy that would require stability in wage rates, and quite aside from the insensitivity of an index of rates of pay, it is doubtful that the use of the latter as a guide to policy would offer, on balance, any distinct advantages over the stabilization of some other price index. The significance of stability of an index of wage rates is likely to be less understandable to the public than one of commodity prices. Perhaps the chief merit of a proposal to stabilize the level of wage rates is that it is useful for expository purposes. Granted the prevailing degree of wage rigidity, it is clear that no less expansionary policy would be defensible. This policy represents, therefore, one of the extreme limits of the range within which a reasonable policy must fall. The other limit is a stabilized wholesale price level, which will be examined shortly.

X

Another price index which would require a secular expansion of the stock of money well within the desirable range is that of retail prices. Inasmuch as these prices would fall relative to wage rates with technological advances, the stabilization of an index of this kind would require a greater expansion in the stock of money than would stabilization of an index of wage rates, and it would, therefore, require some secular advance in money wages with technological innovations. However, an index of this kind, like that of wage rates, would be too insensitive to give the signal for action as promptly as is to be desired if disturbances of considerable magnitude did arise. Nevertheless, it would, in this respect, be superior to a wage index and would not be too impractical to merit adoption if more sensitive indexes could not be made available.

XI

An index of wholesale prices is probably the best guide for monetary action. Most notably, it would be adequately sensitive. It probably would require a greater rate of secular expansion of the stock of money than would a retail index, inasmuch as technological advances are likely to reduce the costs of manufacturing more than those of trading. The possible intensity of a stable-price-level boom would be greater, therefore, if this index were stabilized than would be the case with a stable retail index. However, this is no serious objection. Highly speculative booms of the kind we have encountered under conditions of monetary instability would be unlikely to develop. No boom that is held within the limits of a stable price level will constitute a serious obstacle to the maintenance of a generally high level of output.

XII

There are some further considerations that bear on the question of the best index for stabilization purposes. Goods the prices of which are to be included in the index should be standard commodities. They should be easily definable and their physical characteristics should be stable through time. The use of the prices of specialized commodities which are subject to frequent change would render the index largely meaningless.

It might be supposed that the prices of agricultural commodities should be omitted, despite the fact that these commodities meet very well the requirement of stability in physical characteristics, on the ground that they are subject to price fluctuations caused by variations in supply as well as in aggregate demand. While it is true that crop conditions often cause large variations in the supply of individual commodities, agricultural output as a whole shows a considerable degree of stability.[7]

The aggregate value of the commodities included should be large relative to the national output. If this were not true, a serious departure of prices generally from those in the index would be a real possibility. Stabilization of the prices of relatively unimportant commodities would operate in much the same manner as would a *national* gold standard. It would not stabilize general prices and it would not provide stable foreign exchange rates.

Prices which are included in the index to be stabilized should be flexible. If they are not, the signal for action will be tardy, and not only will the delay in action by the monetary authority permit a disturbance to reach greater proportions, but the confidence of the public will be less, and therefore the need for changes in the stock of money will be greater. Nevertheless, the degree of flexibility required can

[7] For a brief statement relevant to this question see p. 163, note 2.

easily be overemphasized. The wholesale index of the Bureau of Labor Statistics dropped from 98 in September, 1929, to 94 in November and 92 in February, 1930. If we assume a maximum possible spread of six points between the levels at which either expansion or contraction would be initiated, then action after the decline in business conditions in the autumn of 1929 should have been taken certainly no later than the date upon which the February index became available, perhaps within some two weeks after the close of the month. This is on the assumption that the 98 of September, 1929, represented the upper limit of tolerance of the index. If, instead, we assume that the 98 would have been the mid-point in a permitted spread of six points, an increase in the quantity of money would have been called for as soon as the November index became available.

However, any discussion of the timing of action in 1929 or 1930 is in considerable measure meaningless, since it is applying the criteria of a stabilization policy to a historical period when no such policy prevailed. Had there been in effect during the 1920's a known policy of monetary stabilization, the spontaneous action of the public would have resulted in a quite different behavior of the index. Nevertheless, the actual behavior of the index throws some light on the degree of flexibility of an index that might reasonably be expected.

XIII

It may be thought that, inasmuch as small, fortuitous, variations in the price level frequently occur, an attempt to stabilize an index might actually magnify these variations.[8] There must necessarily be some lag between the date upon which monetary action would be indicated by the change in prices and the time at which the action would become

[8] This possibility was suggested by my colleague, Professor Milton Friedman.

effective in the market. Let us assume, for example, that the index declines to the level at which the quantity of money is to be increased, but that without monetary action the price level would have risen again within, say, two months, and that the increase in the quantity of money will likewise not become effective for two months. Under these circumstances, the increase in the quantity of money might so much exaggerate the rise of prices as to bring the index to the level at which contraction would be required. The effect of the withdrawal of money might again coincide with forces that in any event would have reduced the price level. In this way it may seem that an attempt to stabilize an index would or might actually accentuate variations in the level of prices.

If fluctuations in the price level were to be magnified in the above manner to a damaging extent, it would be necessary that there should frequently be a succession of several periods in which the spontaneous and the induced changes in the price level coincided. This is highly improbable. Occasional instances of this kind would merely require that monetary action be reversed, and no great harm would be done. We can possibly obtain some indication of the probability of such a development as this by a historical examination of a price index, although the value of evidence of this kind is limited. To infer that past spontaneous changes in prices would have been the same had there been an established monetary policy instead of the prevailing monetary uncertainty would be unwarranted. Furthermore, in attempting to determine when action should have been taken in the past, we are met with an insurmountable difficulty. Since there was in fact no established monetary norm, historical fluctuations in the index cannot indicate when action should have been taken. We can, however, adopt arbitrary procedures which will not entirely invalidate the evidence.

Let us assume, then, that in each year from 1906 to 1946 we had been attempting to stabilize the index as of January in that year. Let us assume, further, that our policy required action only when the index reached a divergence from the norm (January of each year) of as much as 3 per cent. If we apply this procedure to the monthly wholesale price index of the Bureau of Labor Statistics for these 41 years, we find that there were 32 occasions upon which a change in the quantity of money would have been indicated. Of these, 27 would have been "correct" actions in the sense that in fact the index did not return to the January level within 12 months. This leaves us with five cases in which it superficially appears that action would have been "incorrect." One of these would be removed if we reduce the period to 5 months, and three if it were reduced to 3 months. The time and direction of the indicated changes are shown in Table 8.

TABLE 8. INDICATED CHANGES IN THE STOCK OF MONEY, 1906–1946 *

"Correct" actions				Apparently "incorrect" actions	
November, 1906	−	April, 1926	+	August, 1914	−
June, 1908	+	December, 1929	+	February, 1919	+
September, 1909	−	March, 1930	+	April, 1920	−
April, 1912	−	April, 1931	+	June, 1924	+
October, 1915	−	May, 1932	+	April, 1927	+
March, 1916	−	June, 1933	−		
March, 1917	−	June, 1934	−		
April, 1918	−	December, 1936	−		
July, 1919	−	November, 1937	+		
October, 1920	+	May, 1938	+		
February, 1921	+	May, 1941	−		
April, 1922	−	April, 1942	−		
July, 1923	+	April, 1946	−		
December, 1924	−				

* (−) means a decrease in the quantity of money was indicated by the index in this month, and (+) means an increase was indicated.

The cases of apparently "incorrect" action must be examined further. Manifestly, if the quantity of money in fact changed in the direction required between the month of the indicated change and that in which the index returned to the January level, we should not include such instances with our "incorrect" actions. This was in fact apparently true for three of the five cases.[9] This leaves us with only two "incorrect" actions out of a total of 32. The three cases of changes in the quantity of money in the required direction are February, 1919; June, 1924; and April, 1927. In these instances there was an increase in the quantity of money of 5, 7, and 4 per cent, respectively, within two quarters at the most after a needed increase was indicated.

The apparently genuinely "incorrect" actions were the indicated decreases of August, 1914, and April, 1920. While in these cases the index returned within 2 and 4 months, respectively, to a level below that of January, the quantity of money remained nearly constant. There was a decrease from September 12 to October 31, 1914, of 0.3 per cent, but this is possibly too small a decline to justify us in classifying the action taken in response to the signal given by the index as "correct," although it is at the rate of somewhat more than 2 per cent a year.[10] Between the second and third quarters of 1920 there was an increase of 0.6 per cent.

It is to be remembered that the above analysis of the historical data applies the criteria of an established policy

[9] We must say "apparently," since we do not have monthly statistics, or even quarterly statistics that are entirely satisfactory, for the quantity of money. For the figures prior to 1919 I have used Allyn A. Young's *Analysis of Bank Statistics for the United States* (1928), and for 1919 and thereafter, Clark Warburton's "Quantity and Frequency of Use of Money in the United States," *Journal of Political Economy,* LIV (1946), 436–450.

[10] The figures for 1914 illustrate very nicely the impossibility of obtaining satisfactory data on the quantity of money. The figures for that year include the net individual deposits of national banks plus hand-to-hand currency in circulation outside the banks. Thus deposits of state banks are not included.

to a period during which the only policy was that of maintaining convertibility of all forms of circulating medium into gold. Conditions, however, were such that this expectation gave no promise that extreme fluctuations in the stock of money and the price level would be avoided. We are not justified in assuming that the minor variations in the price level that occurred were the same as those that would have taken place if a policy of stabilizing the price level had prevailed. This fact markedly restricts the value of the evidence of the historical data; but such as it is, it affords no confirmation of the contention that lags in the effectiveness of changes in the stock of money might accentuate fluctuations in the level of prices.

It is also to be remembered that the above analysis does not purport to indicate when or what monetary action should have been taken in the light of the actual conditions that prevailed. "Correct" action in this analysis means merely that the index did not return to the January level within the following 12 months after the index had diverged by 3 per cent from that level; or that, if it did return, it was accompanied by a change in the quantity of money that was in the direction indicated as desirable by the index on the basis of our arbitrary and restricted assumptions. The fact that a reduction in the stock of money was indicated by the index for June, 1933, by no means suggests that in the light of the then existing conditions this would have been desirable monetary action. The sole purpose of this analysis is that of learning what we can about the possibility that a lag in the effectiveness of monetary action would produce harmful consequences.

Chapter 7

THE GUIDE FOR MONETARY ACTION
(Continued)

I

The question that next arises is whether the prices of only domestic or international goods, or both, should appear in an index constructed for the purpose of price-level stabilization. The answer will depend in part upon the monetary system, national or international, that is adopted. It has become almost traditional to say that we may have either fixed exchange rates and a fluctuating price level or flexible exchange rates and a stable price level, but that we cannot have both fixed exchanges and a stable price level. In fact, however, our choice is not quite so restricted as this statement would suggest.

There are two ends, which at times may be difficult to achieve simultaneously, that must be served by a wise monetary policy. (1) Monetary conditions should be provided which will facilitate the necessary internal adjustments in response to international disturbances; and (2) stability of internal monetary conditions should be maintained. If in each country an index of the prices of domestic goods were stabilized under an international gold standard that permitted freedom of gold flows, the effectiveness of the international equilibrating mechanism would be seriously impaired. If, for example, international disequilibrium develops, the mechanism requires a movement of gold and of domestic prices. The efforts of the gold-losing and the gold-gaining countries to stabilize the index would prevent the necessary decline in the prices of domestic relative to international goods in the one case and of their rise in the other, and thus gold would continue to flow until the gold-losing country had lost all its gold.

In the absence of an international disturbance, a policy of stabilizing domestic commodity prices under the gold standard would operate very nicely to prevent the development of unemployment, if in fact the economy continued to show such a degree of instability, despite the policy of monetary stabilization, as to require that deliberate measures be taken to offset disturbances. Any change in business conditions would be reflected in the price index, and thus prompt action could be taken to oppose any untoward developments. Moreover, under conditions of incipient boom or depression, the proper action from the internal point of view would be unlikely to bring about an outflow or an inflow of gold.

Under a one-country-managed gold standard, such as was suggested on pages 108 to 110, stabilization of an index of the prices of domestic goods in the managing country would give more satisfactory results than would an attempt to stabilize such an index, in conjunction with the gold standard, in all countries. The loss or the acquisition of gold by the nonmanaging countries would change their reserve ratios, and there would consequently be a change in the quantity of money and in the prices of domestic goods in those countries. Thus the equilibrating mechanism would function, although primarily in the nonmanaging countries. To some extent, however, the adjustment would take place in the managing country, since as gold flowed out of that country, for example, and the prices of domestic goods therefore began to fall, the quantity of money would be increased. But the other countries would simultaneously also increase the quantity of money in circulation, since their reserves would be rising. Consequently, there would be a world-wide increase in the quantity of money and, therefore, a rise in all countries in the prices of international commodities. Thus there would be a decline in the prices of domestic relative to international goods in the managing country. However, this development would be at the expense of a weakened inducement to make the necessary adjustments in the nonmanaging countries.

This policy would work quite satisfactorily to prevent depressions or booms in the managing country, although possibly not so well in the other countries, since there would be occasions upon which the equilibrating mechanism would require a reduction of wage rates. There would be no possibility of offsetting changes in velocity in the nonmanaging countries, but it is problematical whether this would be a significant drawback. However, the fact of stability in the managing country, in the light of the predominance in foreign trade which it would be required to have, would do much to maintain stability in the other countries.

If the price level of domestic goods were stabilized under a system of flexible foreign exchange rates, the equilibrating mechanism would operate most satisfactorily, while the effectiveness of this policy in maintaining general internal stability in the presence of purely domestic disturbances would be equally good. Inasmuch as the adjusting mechanism would operate by way of a change in exchange rates and in the prices of international goods, the policy would be entirely compatible with the requirements of the mechanism. Of particular importance is the fact that no international disturbance would require a reduction of wage rates. A tendency toward a reduction of output and employment would be reflected in a decline in domestic prices, and the effort to maintain these prices would both sustain aggregate demand and avoid the creation of any international difficulty. This combination of policy and monetary standard merits a high rating from the standpoint of maintaining both external and internal equilibrium.

II

It would be feasible to stabilize the price level of international goods under an international (but, of course, not entirely automatic) gold standard, and herein lies the error in the statement that we cannot have both fixed exchange rates and a stable price level. The adjusting mechanism would be left free to operate in the automatic manner required by the gold standard; that is, there would be no interference with gold flows or with changes in the prices of domestic commodities, with a possible exception noted below. While the mechanism of adjustment would be undisturbed, it nevertheless would require, on occasions, a reduction in wage rates.

Whether this policy would dampen "cyclical" movements as well as would one of stabilizing the prices of domestic goods is uncertain, although it seems likely that it would be less satisfactory in this respect. If a depression began in one country and did not promptly spread to others, there might be no signal given for monetary action to oppose the downward trend of domestic prices and output. There would surely be no such signal if the country were small; but if it were large, the fact of declining prosperity would cause international-goods prices to decline fairly soon, since (1) the demand of the country in question would constitute a significant part of the world demand, and (2) the depression would in fact extend to other countries without much delay. For these reasons the prices of international goods would decline rather soon. On the other hand, no depression in a small country would be likely to become very serious while the remainder of the world continued to be prosperous. By "depression" I am referring to a "cyclical" decline in employment, not to a lower standard of living forced upon a country by the loss of an external market for a major product.

The question arises whether, with this policy, the requirements of the equilibrating mechanism and of antidepression policy might not, on some occasions, be in conflict. Might not a given nation find itself in the position of losing gold and therefore placed under the necessity of reducing domestic prices if its international position was to be reestablished, while at the same time the prices of international goods were falling, in consequence of some measure of world depression? If this situation developed, an increase in the quantity of (convertible) money, called for by the decline in the prices of international goods, would operate to sustain also the prices of domestic goods, and thus the equilibrating mechanism would fail to function in the gold-losing country.

The difficulty arising from this possible dilemma might or might not be serious. No such decline in the prices of international goods could occur in only one country if fixed exchanges prevailed. If a decline did occur, it would be world wide, and consequently other countries would be increasing the quantity of money concurrently with the country losing gold, provided that they also were attempting to stabilize the price level of international goods. Thus in these countries also the prices both of domestic and of international goods would rise, and therefore the mechanism would fail to function there as well as in the gold-losing country. This situation could result in the complete loss of its stock of gold by the latter country if the depression were serious, and if the length of time required to restore the prices of international goods were considerable. However, if the time were relatively short, it might be possible that international prices would be brought back to the "normal" level soon enough to permit the equilibrating mechanism to function, and thus an undue loss of gold would be prevented. Clearly, serious consequences from this conflict between the requirements of the equilibrating mechanism and of antidepression policy would be possible only if monetary stability failed to result at all times in a fairly high level of output. Such failure is very improbable.

If, during a world depression, only the gold-losing country

were attempting to stabilize the price of international goods, while all others were adhering to a purely automatic gold standard, the equilibrating mechanism would function in the same manner as it would were the other countries stabilizing the price level of domestic commodities. However, if the other countries were adhering to an international gold standard but were imposing upon this system the kind of management to which we have been subjected in the past, the results might be disastrous for the one country which was attempting to stabilize the price level of international goods. We have had too much experience with the gold standard, in combination with fractional-reserve banking and discretionary management, to justify any confident expectation that the stock of money would actually be increased with the inflow of gold into the other countries. However, if the gold-losing country chanced to be the dominant country in volume of transactions, the effort of that country alone to maintain the price level of international goods would do much to prevent the depression from reaching major proportions. Nevertheless, one must concede that there might arise this conflict between the requirements of external and internal stability.

This possible dilemma of the monetary authority was recognized by Henry Thornton, although he was not considering the question of a stable price level. It has been frequently discussed since then, but no satisfactory solution has been forthcoming. It should be added, however, that this conflict is not peculiar, under the gold standard, to a policy of stabilizing the price level, and that any difficulty of this sort that might arise would most certainly not lead to more unfortunate consequences than we have frequently witnessed under the operation of the pseudoautomatic gold standard of the past. On the contrary, there is reason to believe that even the attempt by only one (large) country to stabilize the price level of international goods while adhering to a system of fixed exchange rates would lead to far better results than we have known historically; and if all countries were simultaneously following this policy, any conflict between the requirements of external and internal stability would be of minor consequence.

If, under an international gold standard, the price level of international goods were stabilized in each country, national gold reserves might either accumulate in unnecessarily large amounts (conceivably they could exceed 100 per cent) or they might be reduced below the "apprehension minimum," to borrow a term from Walter Bagehot's *Lombard Street*. The former development would create no serious problem, although it would require that an unduly large amount of resources be devoted to gold mining and that there be a surplus of revenues from taxation over ordinary government expenditures. This would not be too much to pay for the benefits derived from stable monetary conditions. Moreover, this cost could be avoided by an increase in the gold content of the currency. However, any such increase should be a matter of international agreement and should be made effective simultaneously and in equal percentages for all gold-standard moneys. If reserves became unduly low—a more likely development—it would be a serious matter and would make urgent a decrease in the content of all gold currencies, again, of course, by international agreement.

Stabilization of the price level of international goods in the managing country, with stable reserve ratios in other countries, would operate in much the same manner under a one-country-managed gold standard as it would under an orthodox gold standard. It probably would be somewhat better, if under the latter system only one country were stabilizing its price level, but not quite so good if all countries were following the same policy. The adjusting mechanism would function in the normal manner—through a decline or a rise in the prices of domestic goods, including wage rates. If a depression began in the managing country, the price level of international goods would decline fairly soon, since the decline in the demand for these goods in the one country, it being of dominant size, would cause the world price level of international goods to decline. Moreover, the depression would quickly spread to other countries if it reached serious proportions in the managing country. For these reasons the latter country would increase the quantity of its circulating medium, while the other countries would not permit a decline in their stocks of money, since a decline would raise their reserve ratios.

Under a national standard, stabilization of the price level of international goods would give better results than it would under either kind of gold standard. The equilibrating mechanism would operate much as it would under the gold standard, but the antidepression effect would be better. If a disturbance caused the exchanges to rise in a given country, the prices of international goods would therefore also rise. This would require a reduction in the quantity of money. The consequence would be not merely to bring the prices of international goods down to their original level, but also to force the prices of domestic goods below their former level. This latter decline is precisely what is required under the gold standard. This policy would give, therefore, substantial stability in exchange rates, although not the complete fixity (within the gold points) of an international standard, inasmuch as stability in the indexes of the prices of international goods in each country would still leave some room for permanent changes in the foreign exchange rates. This would be true because the various national indexes, even though they included the same commodities, would not move precisely together, since the weighting would necessarily not be the same for all the indexes.

Against depressions this policy would operate more satisfactorily than would stabilization of the same index under the gold standard. If a depression began in some one country, regardless of size, the imports of that country would decline fairly soon, and hence both the exchange rates and the prices of international goods would go down. Additional money would therefore be put into circulation without much delay. Furthermore, there would be no danger of crises because of a depletion of the national stock of reserve money.

III

In the preceding discussion of the relative advantages of stabilizing the price level of international and of domestic goods, no account has been taken of the problem of constructing satisfactory index numbers for each of these price levels. In fact, however, it would be impossible to obtain an index number for purely domestic prices that satisfied all the requirements of sensitivity, of importance in the national economy, and of stability of the physical characteristics of the commodities. Unfortunately, under either a national standard or a one-country-managed gold standard, stabilization of the price level of domestic goods would be decidedly preferable to the stabilization of the price level of international goods, and in either of these two cases domestic price-level stabilization would also give promise of better results than the stabilization of the price level of international goods under an international standard. These facts reveal a serious difficulty and suggest the desirability of enquiring into the possible effects of stabilizing a combined index in which the prices of both types of goods are included.

The equilibrating mechanism with stabilization of a combined index under an international gold standard would function in substantially the same manner as it would were the prices of domestic goods alone stabilized under that standard; that is to say, it would work badly. The mechanism requires gold movements and changes in the prices of domestic goods, and the stabilization of an index which included these prices would preclude the possibility of adjustments. The prices of international goods would remain substantially stable as gold movements occurred, and therefore a change in the index because of a change in the prices of domestic goods would require that the latter prices be brought to their original level, very much as if it were an index of the prices of domestic goods alone that was being stabilized. The gold-losing country would offset the loss of gold, and the gold-gaining countries would sterilize the incoming gold. Consequently, there would be no net change in the total stock of money for the world as a whole, and the prices of international goods could not rise. Under these circumstances, the attempts to restore or maintain the indexes would cause a continuance of the gold flow until the losing country had lost all its gold.

On the other hand, this policy would work very satisfactorily in opposition to depression; in fact, somewhat better than stabilization of the price level of international goods under the gold standard. The beginnings of a depression would be reflected early in the decline of the prices of domestic goods, and hence there would be no danger that a decline in output that began in a single country would fail quickly to give the signal for monetary action, as might possibly be the case if the price level of international goods were stabilized.

Stabilization of a combined index would give substantially the same results under a one-country-managed gold standard as would stabilization of the price level of domestic goods alone under the same standard. The equilibrating mechanism would work only fairly well, since the prices of domestic goods would have to decline in a nonmanaging country if the balance of payments were against it. It would function very well in opposition to depressions (or booms), inasmuch as the signal for action would be given promptly in the managing country because of the decline (rise) in the prices of domestic goods, and almost equally promptly reserve ratios would change in any other country in which a depression (boom) might start, thus calling for action to maintain these ratios at their required constant level.

Under a national monetary system and flexible foreign exchange rates, stabilization of a combined index would operate quite as well to avoid depressions, in the unlikely event that such opposition was needed, as would the stabilization of domestic prices; but the equilibrating mechanism would work somewhat less satisfactorily. As output declined in a given country, the prices of domestic goods would surely fall, and probably also the prices of international goods. Thus the signal for action would be given much as it would be were the former prices alone stabilized. On the other hand, if an international disturbance caused the balance of payments to turn against a country, its exchange rate would rise, and therefore also the price level of international goods within that country. This development would require a decrease in the quantity of money and, therefore, a decline in the prices of domestic goods. However, stabilization of a combined index would permit the requisite relative decline in the prices of domestic goods to take place, partly by way of a rise in the prices of international goods, and consequently not so much pressure would be placed upon the prices of domestic goods as would be the case if an index of the prices of international goods alone were stabilized. Fortunately, inasmuch as a combined index could be constructed that would meet the requirements of a good index for purposes of monetary stabilization, this policy would give very satisfactory results—quite the equal of any of the policies we have been discussing in combatting boom or depression, and better in facilitating internal adjustments to an international disturbance than any others, except the stabilization of the price level of domestic goods under a national standard.

Table 9 summarizes in a rough way the above conclusions concerning the relative merits of an index of the prices of international, of domestic, and of both types of goods for stabilization purposes, in combination with different monetary systems.

TABLE 9. OPERATION OF SELECTED MONETARY STANDARDS AND POLICIES

Standard	Stabilization of the price level of international goods		Stabilization of the price level of domestic goods		Stabilization of a combined index	
	Effectiveness of adjusting mechanism	Effectiveness in combatting boom or depression	Effectiveness of adjusting mechanism	Effectiveness in combatting boom or depression	Effectiveness of adjusting mechanism	Effectiveness in combatting boom or depression
National standard	Fair	Good	Very good	Very good	Fair to good	Very good
International gold standard	Fair	Fair to good	Very bad	Very good	Very bad	Very good
One-country-managed gold standard	Fair	Fair to good	Bad to fair	Good	Bad to fair	Good

IV

In the light of all the evidence it appears that the best index of the price level for stabilization purposes would be that of domestic prices, and it would operate best in combination with a national standard. The equilibrating mechanism would function by way of movements in the exchange rates and the prices of international goods, thus making the maintenance of equilibrium with full employment compatible with some downward rigidity of wage rates. However, the impossibility of obtaining a satisfactory index of the prices of domestic goods only constitutes a fatal objection to this policy.

The second-best policy, and the one which should probably be adopted, is that of stabilizing a combined index of the prices of both domestic and international goods under a national standard. The index should be composed of wholesale prices. Wage rates should be excluded. The requirement of wholesale prices grows out of the need for a sensitive index, and out of the desirability that the commodities included be standard and unchanging through time. Wage rates should be excluded because of their rigidity. The equilibrating mechanism would require some reduction of domestic prices when the balance of payments turned against a nation. This fact somewhat reduces the *relative* attractiveness of a national as compared with an international standard, and yet the required decline in the prices of domestic as opposed to international goods could be had partly by way of a rise in the prices of the latter. This fact constitutes a considerable advantage over an international standard.

Appreciably less satisfactory than either of the two preceding policies would be that of stabilizing an index of the prices of international goods under a national standard. The equilibrating mechanism would operate in substantially the same manner as under an international standard, that is to say, the whole weight of adjustment would be thrown on domestic prices. This is the chief reason for giving it a lower rating than a policy of stabilizing an index that is made up wholly or partly of the prices of domestic goods.

Among the more or less acceptable combinations of index to be stabilized and standard to be adopted, that of an index of the prices of international goods and the international gold standard would be least satisfactory. The equilibrating mechanism would operate in the same manner as it would under an automatic gold standard, and also as it would were the same index stabilized under a national standard; but the signal for monetary action in consequence of domestic disturbances would be more delayed than under the latter standard, inasmuch as the exchange rates could not move substantially, and it would be changes in the exchange rates that would cause changes in the prices of international goods under the national standard. Nevertheless, this policy would give fairly good results, and it is to be disparaged chiefly because better policies could be found.

The one thing that should be avoided is an attempt to stabilize an index that includes the prices of domestic goods and at the same time to maintain an international gold standard. Under such circumstances the equilibrating mechanism is made either completely or largely ineffective. How important it is that the mechanism function smoothly we cannot say, although it would seem that in a nation for which foreign trade is large, relative to domestic trade, it would be more important than in one in which the reverse was true. This suggests, it may seem paradoxically, that nations in the former category have as much to gain from the adoption of a national standard as do the latter. To be sure, the fixity of the exchanges under the gold standard is probably conducive to the maximization of trade, other things being equal; but it is doubtful that the favorable effect on trade is large, and it is very doubtful that other things can be equal.

Rapid and as nearly as possible frictionless adjustments to international disturbances, and the maintenance of internal stability, are more important than fixity of the exchange rates; and these can be more nearly achieved with a national standard, particularly if the index to be stabilized includes the prices of domestic goods. The conditions in Great Britain during the 1920's furnish an excellent and compelling illustration of the possible difficulties of fixed exchanges. There can be no reasonable doubt that flexible exchanges and a fair degree of stability of prices would have done much to improve conditions during that decade. Costs were too high for the export industries, but they could not be reduced, nor could the prices of international goods rise in terms of sterling so long as an international standard prevailed and prices were not rising in other countries. Since Great Britain was constantly struggling to avoid a too great loss of gold, it follows that if the exchanges had been free they would have risen, carrying up with them the prices (in terms of sterling only) of British exports.

Under a policy of stabilizing an index of prices in all industrial nations, in combination with flexible exchanges, exchange rates would in fact not vary widely, although the range of fluctuation would be somewhat greater than that permitted by the gold points under a gold standard.

The policy of price-level stabilization would give best results if it were followed by all nations; yet any one nation acting by itself could achieve a high degree of success with such a policy if it maintained a national standard, and so also could any one large nation, even though it adhered to an international gold standard. However, no small nation would be likely, by itself, to be very successful while adhering to an international standard.

V

We must now reexamine the policy of ignoring velocity and increasing the stock of money at some constant rate. If a single nation were following this policy and at the same time maintaining an international gold standard, it would offset losses and possibly, to some extent, acquisitions of gold, and thus would throw the whole burden of adjustment on the other nations. Nevertheless, the necessary adjustments could be made in those nations. If all countries were following the same policy, the losing and possibly the gaining country would offset the gold flow. The stability of the exchange rates would prevent the prices of international goods from changing in response to a change in the international balance of a country, and the failure of the gold flow to change the quantity of money would prevent the prices of domestic goods from changing. Thus there could be no change in the relative prices of domestic and international goods, and consequently the adjusting mechanism would be destroyed completely. This would be true, regardless of the particular rate of increase in the quantity of money that had been adopted.

If some one nation were following the policy of increasing its national currency at a given rate, the policy would operate quite satisfactorily. If the balance of payments turned against that country, the exchange rate would rise, the prices of international goods would therefore rise, and this would require a decline in the prices of domestic goods, since there would be no immediate change in the stock of money. This policy would operate, therefore, in much the same manner as would a policy of stabilizing a combined index under a national standard, which appears to be the best index, for practical reasons, for stabilization purposes.

If all countries were increasing their national currencies at a constant rate, the adjusting mechanism would again operate in much the same manner as would a general policy of stabilizing a combined index. In the country against which the balance of payments turned, developments would be as outlined in the preceding paragraph, while in the other countries, assuming them to be collectively large relative to the country with the unfavorable balance, there would be little or no change in the relative prices of domestic and international goods. This would be for the reason that in the absence of a change in the world demand-and-supply conditions for a given international good, prices for that good in terms of the bulk of the world's currencies would be stable, and thus the whole needed change in relative prices would be imposed on the country with the unfavorable balance. However, if that country were relatively large, some of the adjustment might be thrown on the other countries, since in this case the prices of international goods might decline somewhat in those nations as they rose in the one country. At the worst, therefore, the adjustment would be unilateral.

It now appears that we must somewhat revise our appraisal of the relative merits of stabilizing a price index and of increasing the quantity of money at some constant rate (see p. 123). If an international monetary standard is to be maintained, the adjusting mechanism would be destroyed by a policy of increasing the quantity of money at a given rate if all nations followed that policy, and therefore with such a standard the argument for a price index as the guide to policy is even stronger than it has heretofore appeared to be. If, however, a stable rate of increase is to be associated with a national standard, this policy appears to have no disadvantages whatever, in so far as the adjusting mechanism is concerned, as compared with that of stabilizing a combined index under the same monetary standard. It still remains true, however, that on grounds of maintaining internal stability the policy of stabilizing an index is preferable; but it is also true that a policy of increasing the stock of money at some constant rate would in fact work out very well.

VI

A currency based upon commodity reserves, such as has been proposed by Mr. Benjamin Graham and Professor Frank D. Graham, has much to commend it.[1] It would automatically stabilize the price level of a group of commodities, without fixing individual prices, and at the same time provide an unfailing market for these commodities at this price level. It would, therefore, without question maintain employment and output in the industries producing the commodities included within the reserve, and this fact would further operate in some measure to support prices and output in the other industries. The system would also operate to restrict any rise in prices brought on by an increase in velocity, since the reserves would be drawn upon, and in this way the stock of money would be contracted, when the market price of the reserve commodities rose above the official selling price. Furthermore, the system

[1] I have been greatly assisted in my analysis of the commodity reserve system by an incidental discussion of the subject with Messrs. Aaron Director, Milton Friedman, F. A. Hayek, and Russell Nichols.

would operate automatically, which is no minor consideration. Nevertheless, it is doubtful that these very real advantages are sufficient to offset the serious shortcomings of the system.

If there were a secular rise in the volume of output of the economy, the commodity-reserve system would operate constantly to increase the amount of the commodity reserves, since the downward pressure on the price level would keep the market price of the reserve commodities as a group at or near the official buying price most of the time. If we assume the rate of growth in output to be 3½ per cent a year, the value of commodities immobilized in the reserves during a period of 20 years would equal the stock of money at the beginning of the period. If the system were instituted at the present time, therefore, the value of commodities drawn into the reserves during the next 20 years would reach $110 billion. To be sure, under an automatic, nonfractional-reserve gold standard the value of gold withdrawn would also be great, although possibly not so great in dollar value, inasmuch as stabilization of the price of gold under a nonfractional-reserve standard might not maintain the general level of prices. Nevertheless, the amount of resources used in producing this gold might be as great.

One is tempted to look upon the withdrawal of such commodities as would be found in the commodity reserves as much more unfortunate than the withdrawal from use of an equal value of gold, but there is no real difference. The significant consideration is not the nature of the commodities of which we deny ourselves the use, but rather the fact that the resources used in producing the monetary reserves, whether gold or other commodities, might have been devoted to the production of goods for current consumption or capital creation. To a minor extent, this disadvantage could be lessened by including in the stock of money a fixed amount of fiduciary currency. This device, however, could operate only to reduce the amount of reserve commodities needed to initiate the system, since thereafter all new money would have to be obtained from the monetization of commodities (or gold). It would, of course, be possible to continue the issuance of fiduciary money indefinitely in some fractional ratio to the total stock of money, but such a procedure would eliminate the completely automatic character of the system, one of its more important attractions.

The chief advantage of the commodity-reserve system, as compared with the gold standard, would arise from the supposed possibility of including in the monetary reserves commodities whose annual output had an aggregate value large in relation to the quantity of money. Failure to achieve this high aggregate value would mean that, in order to obtain a sufficient change in the stock of money adequately to oppose a rise or a fall in the price level, a very pronounced effect on the prices of reserve commodities relative to those of other commodities, and large reallocations of resources would be necessary. Any influence of the monetary system per se on relative prices and the allocation of resources is undesirable, and it is also unnecessary that we resort to a system which exercises such an influence. In fact, however, as will be pointed out presently, the possibility of a high aggregate value of the annual output of reserve commodities is largely illusory.

It would also be desirable that the weight of each commodity in the reserves be lower than its relative importance in the output of the reserve commodities, since if this were true, monetization and withdrawal of commodities would have less effect on relative prices and allocation of resources. But manifestly this is impossible, since if one commodity is given a low weight, some other or others must be given correspondingly higher weights.

Inelasticity of either demand or supply for a given reserve commodity would have unfortunate consequences. If the (price) elasticity of demand for some one reserve commodity were low, the result would be a marked change in the price of the commodity when monetization or withdrawal took place. This would mean that adequate changes in the stock of money could take place only when the prices of the other reserve commodities had changed sufficiently to offset the rise or the fall in the price of the commodity in question. The consequence would be a sharp limitation on the extent of changes in the quantity of money. In any case, the influence of the monetary system on relative prices would be pronounced.

If elasticity of supply were low, the effects would be much the same as those of a low elasticity of demand. These effects can be clearly seen if we consider the case of a bumper or a short crop of some one agricultural reserve commodity. The monetary system would have no effect on conditions unless monetization or withdrawal were concurrent with the unusual crop conditions. Quite the contrary would be true, however, if, for example, a bumper crop of one product coincided with a period of withdrawals from the reserves. In this case the consequence would be a drastic decline in the price of the product, which would be reinforced by a presumably low elasticity of demand in the case of a staple agricultural product.

It may be thought that, if agricultural products constituted the major element in the commodity reserves, the effect of the system would be to prevent those desirable fluctuations in price which operate to spread the consumption of the crop, whether large or small, over the period between crops. Upon examination, however, it turns out that this effect would not be present. If, for example, a bumper crop came at a time when monetization was taking place, the weakening effect on the prices of agricultural products would tend to increase the extent and to prolong the process of monetization. While, therefore, the monetary system would have the direct effect of preventing a fall in the actual prices of agricultural products, the essential relative decline would, nevertheless, be obtained through a rise in the prices of other products in consequence of the pronounced increase in the stock of money. Moreover, the opposition to deflation that was currently taking place would be strengthened.

If bumper crops coincided with withdrawals of reserve commodities, both the large crops and the operation of the monetary system would tend to reduce the relative prices of agricultural products, and thus the consumption of the large stocks during the following year would be promoted. However, the tendency for agricultural prices to fall might either immediately or shortly put a stop to the process of withdrawal, and thus the opposition to inflation would be somewhat weakened.

By similar analyses it can be shown that the coincidence of short crops and monetization would permit the relative prices of agricultural products to rise and thus to induce a lower rate of consumption, while the opposition to deflation would be weakened. The concurrence of short crops and withdrawals of commodities would again permit a rise in the relative prices of agricultural products, and it would strengthen the opposition to inflation. Granted the agricultural products included in the reserves were internationally traded goods, as they preponderantly would be, the above results would obtain whether the commodity-reserve system were adopted internationally or by one country only. However, in the latter case, a bumper crop in conjunction with monetization would result in a somewhat stronger opposition to deflation than would obtain under an international commodity-reserve system. In this case, indeed, such a conjuncture might even institute a minor deflation. Similarly, bumper crops during withdrawals would weaken the opposition to inflation; short crops during monetization would result in a weaker opposition to deflation; and short crops during withdrawals would bring about a stronger opposition to inflation and might even institute a minor period of deflation.[2]

[2] Index numbers of total crop production per acre of cropland for the United States (1935–1939=100) from 1919 to 1944 reveal clearly the improbability of frequent and concurrent large or small crops in

It should also be noted that if short crops coincided with monetization the welfare effects would be unfortunate. Furthermore, there would be little or no short-term employment effect in agriculture to be derived from the inclusion of agricultural commodities. This, however, is not a positive disadvantage; it is merely an absence of any desirable effect. The above considerations make it very doubtful that agricultural products should be included among the reserve commodities, and yet from the standpoint of their physical characteristics and their aggregate value they are among the most suitable for this purpose. If they are excluded, about the only suitable commodities left are minerals. Restriction of the reserves to these would give rise to the disadvantage of an unduly small aggregate value of the yearly output of the reserve commodities relative to the stock of money. The danger would then arise that additions to or subtractions from the stock of money would be insufficient to prevent an undue change in the prices and output of nonreserve commodities.

VII

The preceding discussion has been based upon the assumption that the stock of money would be controlled exclusively by the operations of the commodity-reserve system. It would be feasible, however, to combine a policy of price-level stabilization by means of monetary measures with the commodity-reserve plan. If I interpret them correctly, this statement is not in conflict with the position of the Messrs. Graham. Resort to commodity reserves as an aux-

---

the aggregate and either monetization or withdrawal of reserve commodities. Between 1919 and 1932 the index varied between 94 and 108, with only one year as low as 94 and only one as high as 108. The index fell to 89 in 1933, 73 in 1934, and 81 in 1936. Following 1936 the index rose sharply, but fairly consistently. See Glen T. Barton and Martin R. Cooper, *Farm Production in War and Peace* (U.S. Department of Agriculture, Bureau of Agricultural Economics), p. 84.

iliary device for implementing monetary policy, however, would have a bearing on the nature of the index to be stabilized. It would not be feasible to include in the commodity reserve as many commodities as would be desirable in the index. There would, therefore, be a possibility of a divergence between the price level of the reserves and of the commodities in the index. The prices of the reserve commodities should, of course, be included within the index, both because doing so would decrease the probability of this divergence, and because they would be precisely the kind of commodities that would answer best the requirements for a good index.

If monetary policy and the commodity-reserve system were combined, each could and should be permitted to function independently of the other. This would mean that the monetary authority would be guided solely by the behavior of the index, without regard to the size of, or the current rate of increase or of decrease in the volume of, the commodity reserves. On the other hand, the commodity-reserve system should be permitted to function at all times in a completely automatic manner. This independence of operation could lead to conflicting tendencies in the two controlling factors over the monetary stock only if conditions of equilibrium required a change in the relative price levels of the two groups of commodities. One of the two possible divergences might lead to a continuing conflict of this kind, but the other, at worst, to a temporary conflict only.

If conditions so changed that equilibrium required the price level of reserve commodities to fall relative to the index by as much as the difference between the buying "price" of the commodities and the upper limit of tolerance of the index, it would become necessary for the monetary agency continuously to withdraw money from circulation, while the commodity-reserve system would continuously add to the stock of money. The consequence would be an unending increase in the volume of commodity reserves, and thus a large volume of resources would be allocated to the production of commodities to be uselessly impounded. Whether this contingency arose would depend upon the extent and direction of the divergence between the price levels, upon the spread between the buying and selling "prices" for the reserve commodities, and upon the limits of tolerance for the index.

If, on the other hand, equilibrium required a relative decline in the index, commodities might no longer be offered for conversion, inasmuch as the monetary agency would add to the stock of money sufficiently to maintain the index, and thus the market "price" of a unit of commodity reserves would always be above the official buying "price." If the market "price" rose above the selling "price," the existing reserves would be withdrawn, thereby tending to reduce the stock of money while the index was still below the upper limit of tolerance and conceivably at the lower limit at which the monetary agency would add to the stock of money. However, such a conflict would last only until the reserves were exhausted. Thereafter, the commodity-reserve system would cease to function, except that if a depression reached considerable proportions the price level might again drop to the point at which monetization of commodities would take place. This failure of the system to operate until depression appeared would constitute no major disadvantage.

Because of the possibility of a divergence between the price level of the commodity reserves and the index, it would be desirable to provide in advance for a revision, if needed, in the "price" of the reserve commodities. Such revisions might never become necessary and, if they did, the need would surely be very infrequent. The stabilization of an index of prices by means of monetary measures would provide the necessary certainty of monetary conditions, and therefore infrequent changes in the official buying and selling "prices" of the reserve commodities could have no significant, untoward consequences.

It would be possible to retain a place for gold in combination with the commodity-reserve system. This could be done either by maintaining a constant buying price for gold, as at present, or by including gold as one of the commodity reserves and giving it a high weighting. The former procedure would create a system somewhat similar to a bimetallic standard and might require occasional changes in the buying price for gold. The latter would not, of course, give the complete fixity of exchange rates of the orthodox gold standard.

While the commodity-reserve system could be successfully operated in combination with some other monetary policy, a hybrid of this kind offers no positive advantages. On the other hand, it would retain to some extent the undesirable influence of the pure commodity-reserve system on relative prices, and it would constitute a degree of complexity in monetary arrangements that should by all means be shunned. In monetary affairs simplicity in objective, organization, and procedure is of the first importance.

VIII

Professor Milton Friedman and the Committee for Economic Development have recently made independent proposals for stability in the tax rates and expenditures of the Federal government during *fluctuations* in employment and output.[3] In the form in which the proposal is made by Friedman it would be a reasonably satisfactory alternative to increasing the stock of money at some constant rate or of stabilizing the price level, although, to my mind, it is nevertheless somewhat inferior to either of these procedures. The proposal of the Committee for Economic Development leaves out essential elements that are included

[3] Milton Friedman, "A Monetary and Fiscal Framework for Economic Stability," *American Economic Review,* XXXVIII (1948), 245–264; Committee for Economic Development, *Taxes and the Budget* (1947).

in the Friedman draft, with the consequence that it would be much less promising.

Friedman's proposal contains four elements: (1) It would eliminate fractional-reserve banking and discretionary control of the stock of money by a central bank. (2) It would stabilize the volume of Federal expenditures on goods and services during fluctuations in business activity, transfer payments being excluded. Changes in the level of expenditures would be permitted, but only in so far as the value attached to such expenditures by the public should change. (3) There would be a definite schedule of expenditures for relief and other transfer payments. (4) Federal revenues would be obtained primarily from a progressive income tax, the rate structure of which would not be changed in response to fluctuations in business activity. Rates would be set originally so as to balance the budget at a high level of employment, and thereafter would be unchanged except as the community desired to change the level of public expenditures or transfer payments. If such changes were made, the rate structure would be so changed as to balance the budget again at a high level of employment.

The objective of the Friedman proposal is to eliminate discretionary action in adjusting the stock of money to fluctuations in business activity. If employment fell off, revenues would decline and the deficit would be met by newly created money. This addition to the stock of money would oppose the decline in employment. If inflation developed, revenues would rise and the surplus would be impounded. Open-market activities would be eliminated.

It should be emphasized that the elimination of fractional-reserve banking is essential to the automatic operation of the Friedman proposal. If banks were retained it is at least possible that they would at times expand or contract the volume of their assets to such an extent and with such rapidity as to outrun the automatic surpluses and deficits of the budget. It should also be noted that this proposal implies flexible foreign exchange rates.

Under the stable-budget policy the international equilibrating mechanism would operate in much the same manner as would a policy of stabilizing an index made up of the prices of both international and domestic goods. As the balance of payments moved against a country, the prices of international commodities would rise and those of domestic commodities would fall, but not so much as under an international standard. This operation of the mechanism we have found to be the best that is practically possible, and consequently our conclusion must be that this proposal merits as high a rating as any feasible alternative from the standpoint of its effectiveness in maintaining international equilibrium.

How well would the Friedman budget proposal stabilize the expectations of the public? This is an unanswerable question in the absence of experience, and yet our appraisal of the policy must rest on an answer. If a boom or a depression developed, the stock of money would decline in the one case and rise in the other. The public would therefore be assured that either depression or boom would be automatically opposed, and knowledge of this element of monetary stability would do much to provide for an autonomous maintenance of a generally high level of output. The extent of any deficit or surplus is not precisely predictable, but we may gain some rough idea of its probable magnitude by observing the effect of the decline in incomes on income tax liabilities for the years 1930 and 1931. Despite a slight increase in effective rates, liabilities under the personal income tax fell from $1,002 million in 1929 to $477 million in 1930, a decline of 52 per cent; and they fell further to $246 million in 1931, an additional decline of 48 per cent. This deficit in 1930 by itself would have provided for an increase in the stock of money (demand deposits and hand-to-hand currency) of $525 million, or 2 per cent of the $26, 366 million outstanding on December

31, 1929. This is not a very impressive figure, and yet if there had been this increase, instead of the actual decrease of $1,794 (7 per cent), which took place during the year 1930, business conditions would have been vastly better than in fact they were. Furthermore, under the changed conditions of the Federal budget which are likely to prevail in the future, a much larger deficit, in terms of a percentage of the stock of money, would arise from a decline in incomes comparable with that of 1930.

Individual income taxes withheld during the fiscal year ending June 30, 1947, were $9,842 million, and other individual income tax collections for the same period were $9,501 million—a total of $19,343 million. This latter figure does not represent precisely the tax *liabilities* for the fiscal year 1947, but it is not incorrect by a large amount, since the corresponding figures for 1946 were nearly the same. If we apply the 52 per cent reduction in liabilities of the year 1930 to this $19,343 million, we obtain a possible deficit with fixed rates and expenditures for 1947 of $10,058 million. We cannot know whether the deficit would actually be greater or less than this amount, since there is a factor that would operate to make it greater and another to make it less. The more progressive rates which were in effect in 1947, as compared with those of 1930, would mean that, as incomes decreased, the effective rate would be reduced more rapidly in the later than in the earlier year. This would tend to make the deficit greater than $10,058 million. But exemption levels were lower in 1947 than in 1930, and this means that tax collections would decline more at the lower end of the income scale in 1930 than in 1947, since a larger number of persons would be relieved of tax liabilities altogether. Nevertheless, this estimate does give us some idea of the order of magnitude of the decline in income tax liabilities. Furthermore, there were no transfer payments in 1930. With a decline in employment at the present time these payments would rise and would further increase the deficit. Finally, other tax collections would also decline with a decrease in incomes. Probably, therefore, a decline in incomes in 1947 comparable with that of 1930 would have produced a deficit in excess of the indicated reduction of $10,058 million in income tax liabilities. The $10,058 million would itself have provided for an increase in the stock of money of 9 per cent, inasmuch as the volume of demand deposits and hand-to-hand currency stood at $109 billion on June 30, 1947.

The above analysis indicates that the automatic responses of the budget under the stable-budget plan would be of significant magnitude. Nevertheless, they would not necessarily be any more nearly of the "right" amount than would open-market operations under a policy of stabilizing a price-level index. Likewise, the lag in response to the budget deficits and surpluses would not be less unfortunate than similar lags might be with open-market operations. Furthermore, a policy of increasing the quantity of money at a constant rate or of stabilizing a price-level index, could and should also be associated with a policy of short-run stability in expenditures, and in practice probably tax rates as well, although formal provision for rate variation might desirably be made as a means of increasing confidence in the program. If rates were in fact varied, the variation would undoubtedly be of the kind to increase automatic deficits and surpluses.

Monetary stabilization is needed as one of the rules of a competitive society. It is needed to prevent undue fluctuations in the expectations of the business community. For this purpose stability in the general level of prices is the essential requirement. Any alternative rule that may be adopted should be preferred only because of some difficulty in implementing a policy of stabilizing the price level, and the alternative itself should promise no serious departure from price-level stability. The possible difficulties that might be encountered in price-level stabilization are two: (1) the lag in the effect of monetary action, and (2) the discretionary power that would have to be given to some administrative official in regard to the amount of open-market operations. Friedman's proposal does nothing to overcome the first of these difficulties, and while it eliminates the second, it substitutes a device which would leave the extent of monetary action quite as uncertain as it would be with discretionary power over the amount of open-market operations. A constant rate of addition to the stock of money would provide for this needed certainty with respect to the amount of money added to the system and, in this way, would be preferable to the stable-budget policy. Since the effect of the latter policy on the price level would not be easily understandable, it would be less acceptable, as far as this aspect of the problem is concerned, than stabilization of the price level. It would also have unfortunate secular effects, which will be considered in Chapter 9. Nevertheless, the stable-budget policy, in the form of Friedman's proposal, must be accepted as one of several reasonably satisfactory rules of monetary policy from which a choice can be made.

The Committee for Economic Development would fix tax rates to yield approximately a $3 billion surplus, with unemployment at about 4 per cent of the labor force. They would then, like Friedman, keep these rates unchanged during fluctuations in the level of employment. They would also oppose any marked attempt to vary expenditures, other than transfer payments, with inflation and deflation, although some minor variations they would permit.[4]

In a later statement, the Committee have added to their original proposal their recommendations on monetary policy in the sense of central-bank action. Whereas in *Taxes and the Budget* they gave the impression that they were attempting to formulate a policy which would be entirely or largely automatic in operation, in their later statement they substantially forsake this point of view. They retain the stable budget, but in addition they now recommend

[4] Committee for Economic Development, *Taxes and the Budget: a Program for Prosperity in a Free Economy* (1947), pp. 28–34.

action by the central bank which is entirely discretionary as to the guide for action and the kind and extent of action. When inflation threatens, they would have the central bank buy government bonds from the banks, raise the rediscount rate, or increase reserve requirements. In inflation this procedure would be reversed.[5] Nevertheless, despite their reference to inflation and deflation, they do not recommend that the price level be the sole or the chief guide for action, nor do they propose any other one specific criterion. They merely ask that monetary policy be directed toward the maintenance of economic stability. Their belief in discretionary management is underlined by the following statement:[6]

> In making its decisions it will be necessary for the Federal Reserve to take into account conditions in particular markets as reflections of, or influences upon, the over-all situation. But concern with particular markets should not be allowed to interfere with action required by the state of the whole economy.

The Committee's recommendations on open-market policy conform to past practice and traditional attitudes, that is to say, they would buy government bonds in booms from the proceeds of taxation, but from the banks; and they would sell to the banks in depression. To my mind this is precisely the reverse of a reasonable use of open-market powers. Purchases should be made in depression with newly created money, but from nonbankers; and sales should be made to nonbankers in booms, the proceeds of the sales being impounded.

[5] Committee for Economic Development, *Monetary and Fiscal Policy for Greater Economic Stability* (1948), pp. 36–37.

[6] *Ibid.*, p. 46.

Chapter 8

THE IMPLEMENTATION OF MONETARY POLICY

I

The institutional arrangements that are deemed to be desirable or essential for the implementation of monetary policy will vary with one's position on monetary matters. There can be distinguished four points of view which have determined opinions on this question: (1) that the monetary agency or authority, of whatever character it may be in other respects, should be independent of political influence; (2) that a monetary "authority" invested with discretionary power is an essential requirement, those who take this position looking upon a central bank as the most suitable instrument for monetary management; (3) that all discretionary action in regard to the currency should be avoided, a point of view to which the international gold standard, Friedman's proposal, and the commodity-reserve system conform; and (4) that "management" of the stock of money should be in accordance with some definitely announced rule, and that discretionary power should be reduced to the lowest possible minimum. Those who hold these opinions agree, therefore, that automaticity is desirable, but they cannot see that any completely automatic currency system is possible which will achieve all that might be gained from nondiscretionary management. They necessarily concede that in respect to the *extent* of action required some discretion is unavoidable, but they deny that the occasion for action must or should be left to the judgment of one or more men.

The preceding points of view are not in all cases mutually exclusive. For example, those who hold that discretionary management is desirable for the most part also object to political influence in monetary matters; and manifestly those who defend an automatic currency must likewise object to political influence.

II

Before the Civil War there were many defenders of a so-called "hard" money, a money consisting of coins only. These men objected to political influence over the stock of money. Their point of view was reflected in the passage of the Independent Treasury acts of 1840 and 1846 in the United States, and a quite similar position was responsible for Peel's Act of 1844 in Great Britain. They were sometimes confused on the subject of bank deposits. In England the currency school held that the stock of hand-to-hand currency should vary automatically and precisely as though it were made up solely of coins; but these men either wholly misunderstood the nature of bank deposits or greatly underestimated their importance. In the United States there was the same confusion on the part of many writers, and yet some few recognized that their proposals logically required the elimination of the commercial banks. William M. Gouge and Charles H. Carroll, in particular, were so strongly of this opinion that their criticisms of the banks were extremely caustic.

While a genuinely automatic international gold standard has much to commend it, the current popular faith in gold grows not out of an understanding of it, but out of misunderstanding and tradition. Of its several advantages only that of its consistency with a balanced budget is widely understood. The blind attachment of the public to gold, in combination with the general lack of understanding of the perverse monetary influence of the banks, has without much doubt been largely responsible for the failure to achieve a more nearly adequate conception of the function of monetary policy in a competitive society.

Among its commendatory features an international gold standard would provide fixed foreign exchange rates, although this cannot be considered a matter of major importance. Of more significance, such a standard, if fractional-reserve bank money were completely eliminated, would provide for some annual increase in the stock of money; and the rate of increase, even though not at the most desirable level, would nevertheless be reasonably stable and predictable for several years in advance. It would, therefore, give in considerable measure that definiteness which is a prime essential of monetary policy. Furthermore, an automatic metallic standard would not require that discretionary power be given to a nonlegislative body, and it would permit a balanced budget at all times. However, if an automatic international standard is to operate at all satisfactorily, it is of paramount importance that fractional-reserve banking be eliminated and that free markets, internally and internationally, be maintained. The further actual conditions diverge from the ideal for the functioning of the monetary system, the less relatively attractive this standard becomes.

III

The second group of opponents of political influence—at the opposite extreme to that of the "hard"-money enthusiasts—are those writers, reaching back to Adam Smith, who have contended that the operations of the commercial banks, if they are confined to the making of short-term, commercial loans, will automatically provide for the appropriate variations in the quantity of money. Long experience with the banks should have demonstrated by now, if theory could not, that this position is unsound. Nevertheless, many

American writers still adhere to this point of view, although it has apparently substantially disappeared in Great Britain. We are not, however, required to base our disbelief in this position upon experience alone. The essential error in this real-bills doctrine is the contention that basing the money on the *money value* of some kind of economic good will limit its quantity. When it is proposed that the quantity of money be made to depend upon the value of some commodity, the unsoundness of the proposal has usually been recognized; but for some very strange reason it has not been so frequently understood that money which is related in quantity to the money value of some kind of credit instrument arising out of business transactions suffers from precisely the same shortcoming.[1] Granted the soundness of their analysis of the operations of commercial banking, it is evident that the defenders of the real-bills doctrine would have been justified in their contention that the banks, if left to themselves, or at the most, if they were required to restrict their loans to short-term, commercial purposes, would automatically regulate the quantity of money in accordance with the "needs of business." Such a system, therefore, would have avoided the necessity either for any other monetary institutions than the banks themselves or for any political control of the stock of money, although it could not have eliminated the ultimate power of the legislature over the monetary system.

IV

The third type of proposal for supposedly nonpolitical control of the stock of money comes from those who look upon central banks as desirable or essential monetary agen-

[1] It is, of course, true that the aggregate value of the commodity eligible as security for money, or of the eligible credit instruments, might be such, under equilibrium conditions, as to limit the issuance of money; but the probability that such conditions would ever be encountered is infinitesimally small.

cies, but who contend that such institutions should be entirely independent of governmental influence. Moreover, they would grant to the central bank complete freedom to determine what its policy should be, or to refrain from deciding upon any specific or announced policy.

The belief that monetary stability can be achieved by means of changes in the discount rate of a central bank originated with Henry Thornton. He enunciated the doctrine that the Bank of England could control the volume of its lending by means of appropriate variations in its discount rate, granted that the usury laws had permitted, before Parliamentary committees in 1797, and again in his *Enquiry into the Nature and Effects of the Paper Credit of Great Britain,* published in 1802. This belief grew slowly in Great Britain, until approximately 1860, while it was almost nonexistent in the United States before that date. During the second half of the nineteenth century, British writers exhibited greater faith in the efficacy of central bank rate, although there was a near absence of suggestions that it might be used to stabilize either business conditions or the price level. About all that was expected of bank rate was that it would enable the Bank of England to protect its reserves from undue drains of gold and thus to avoid panics.

Within the brief period of some dozen years following the First World War, the opinion that bank rate might be a means, not merely of protecting reserves, but of stabilizing either business activity or the general level of prices or both, became, if I am not mistaken, predominant among economists and central bankers. Then with amazing rapidity the doctrine lost defenders during the 1930's.

The experience of the thirties offers no adequate basis for this partial repudiation. The discount rate of the New York Federal Reserve Bank was gradually reduced from 6 per cent in October, 1929, to 1½ per cent in May, 1931; while the buying rate on bills was reduced during the same period of time from 5⅛ per cent to 1 per cent. Moreover, the first reductions came promptly after the stock-market panic of October, 1929, the buying rate on bills being reduced on October 25 and the discount rate on November 1. Nevertheless, even though initial reductions were prompt, the later easing of the rate was very gradual; and there were sharp, although temporary, increases in October, 1931, and in March, 1933. Furthermore, the Reserve System did not support its rate policy with open-market purchases. The total earning assets of the 12 banks decreased from $1,600 million at the end of October, 1929, to $900 million in August, 1931. Thereafter there was an increase to $2,200 million in October of the same year; but again decline set in, with the total falling to $1,600 million in March, 1932. This was precisely the amount of October, 1929.

If discount rates had been reduced not only promptly, but sharply, and—of much more importance—if open-market purchases had been made in such amounts as to increase markedly the total earning assets of the Reserve Banks, and if under these circumstances the depression had progressed substantially as it did from 1929 to 1932, one might then perhaps cite such facts as evidence against the effectiveness of central-bank action. In fact, however, there was essentially a passive attitude on the part of the Reserve System at a time when it should have shown the utmost aggressiveness. Clearly there was nothing but confusion, irresolution, and an appalling lack of understanding of their responsibilities by the officials of the Reserve System and the government. Under these circumstances a defender of central banking can present a devastating reply to those who offer the experience of the thirties in criticism of his position.

Furthermore, even though a reasonable policy had been followed after the panic of 1929 and depression had not then been avoided, the critics of central-bank action would find doubtful ground for their position in the fact that depression developed. If monetary policy, however implemented, is to be effective, it must be in accordance with an established and publicly announced program of action. At the time of the panic no such policy had been announced. It was therefore entirely reasonable to anticipate the inaction and confusion that prevailed during 1930 and 1931, and this fact would have made the task of the monetary agency difficult, even though rational measures had been taken.

The critics of monetary policy, and I am not now referring merely to the disbelievers in central banking, are prone to contend that it would have been difficult or impossible in 1932 and 1933 to restore equilibrium by monetary measures. Such a contention reveals a total lack of understanding of the position of those who ask for a policy of monetary stabilization. The critics must show, not that heroic measures were required in 1932 and 1933, but that action taken early in 1930, in accordance with an established policy, would not have prevented the development of a major depression. This tendency to revert to the difficulties of successful action in 1932 and 1933 and to ignore the absence of preventive action before those years, as well as the absence of an established policy under which action would have been required, is so persistent that I am puzzled by it. What could or could not have been done in the depths of the depression is irrelevant in the discussion of a policy of monetary stabilization, since it must necessarily be admitted that if such conditions did develop, despite a policy which purported to maintain stability, the policy itself would have to be declared a failure. What should one think of the driver of an automobile who, when beginning the descent of a steep hill, refused to use his brakes, and who later declared that brakes were of no value, since he could not stop the car?

Those who would rely upon bank rate for purposes of monetary control recognize the truth of many of the foregoing criticisms and of those presented in Chapter 1. They hope, nevertheless, by means of indirect control of the "member" banks, to offset their undesirable actions and to induce them at times to take more positive steps in the direction desired by the central institution. Since central banks have open-market powers, which are vastly more important than the power of manipulating a rediscount rate upon borrowings by the "member" banks, we might accept such institutions as monetary agents if the extent of the criticism of them were that they could not adequately control the operations of the "member" banks by their open-market and rediscount powers. But there are other grounds for opposition to central banks.

The position of the proponents of central banks that are independent of governmental influence is a strange one. They must realize that any central institution will be the creature of the legislature. What, then, do they mean by political independence? As a minimum they apparently mean that the central bank should be legally independent of the administrative branch of the government. Consistently with this point of view the legislature has sometimes placed a limit upon the amount that the Treasury might borrow from the central bank. It is possible, however, that they would also hold it to be important that the Treasury *voluntarily* refrain from any attempt to influence, informally or extralegally, the actions of the central institution. Their statements on this point are not explicit.

In the final analysis, independence of a central bank is an impossibility. Even though it may legally ignore completely the treasury department of the government, the fact that it will in practice act in accordance with the desires of that office during times of emergency has been amply demonstrated by history. It is inconceivable that it should be otherwise. Furthermore, even though independence of this kind were attainable, the legislature would always be in a position to intervene if it disapproved of the actions or policies of the banks.

Nevertheless, the fatal objection to a central bank lies neither in the impossibility of protecting it from political influence nor in its alleged impotence. Singleness of purpose in monetary affairs is of paramount importance, but numerous agencies of control beget confusion, irresponsibility, and conflicting action, instead. Central banks represent at best a second monetary agency, since operations of the treasury department of necessity have monetary significance. To establish some speciously independent agency to manage the monetary affairs of the country is to delude ourselves into believing that fiction is fact. The deception includes the legislators themselves, the Treasury, and the general public. Thus the real responsibility of the legislature and of the Treasury is understood by no one. We are not likely to get reasonable monetary action from public officials who are uncontrolled by any precise mandate from the legislature and who are unaware of the extent of their responsibility in monetary matters.

V

The monetary-institutional structure of the United States reflects the wide variety of opinion on this subject. Legislation at one time will reflect predominantly a given point of view; at another, a quite different one. In the end, institutions and legislative regulations have emerged which are fundamentally inconsistent. Thus the Federal Reserve Act reveals the influence of the real-bills doctrine, but nevertheless we inconsistently retain a semblance of adherence to the gold standard. However, we also grant to the Board of Governors of the Federal Reserve System wide discretionary powers. Surely the supposed automaticity of the real-bills basis for monetary control, the genuine automaticity (as it might be) of the international gold standard, and the discretionary powers of the Board of Governors are as sharply incompatible in point of view as they could be. Nevertheless, the influence of each is revealed in existing legislation.

We have a ludicrous number of agencies possessed of some measure of monetary authority in the United States today. The final authority is Congress. Legislation determining whether there is to be a balanced budget, a surplus or a deficit, and if the latter, the manner of meeting it is a major determinant of the stock of money. Aside from this legislation Congress is usually quiescent on the subject of money, and it is therefore easy to infer that it has no part in the implementation or formulation of monetary policy. However, when conditions become chaotic, Congress invariably becomes legislatively active in a way that should make its exclusive authority in these matters evident to all. One need cite only such outstanding acts as those providing for the issuance of greenbacks during the Civil War; for the purchase of silver; for the devaluation of the gold dollar in 1934; for recurrent changes in tariff schedules and the creation, extinction, or reorganization of such monetary agencies as the Independent Treasury, the Federal Reserve System and the Federal Deposit Insurance Corporation.

The Secretary of the Treasury unavoidably has large monetary powers. He is the chief monetary agent of Congress. This fact alone, therefore, means that if there is a central bank not under the control of the Treasury Department there will be as a minimum two agencies acting under the authority of the legislature; and two such agencies, acting at cross purposes, can produce about as much chaos as a larger number could. To be sure, experience shows that under conditions that are deemed to be critical the Treasury will invariably exhibit the greater powers of "persuasion." The Secretary is the manager of the fiscal affairs of the government, and presumably he has some influence in determining the nature of fiscal legislation. Currently he can purchase silver and issue silver certificates therefor, and he can engage in open-market operations.

Legally independent of the Treasury is the Board of Governors of the Federal Reserve System. Its members can determine discount rates of the Federal Reserve banks; they define eligibility of paper for rediscount; they, in effect, have control of the managing personnel of the Federal Reserve banks; and, within limits, they can determine the reserve requirements of member banks.

Semi-independent of the Board is the Federal Open Market Committee, which consists of the seven members of the Board of Governors and five members elected by the Federal Reserve banks. The Board would therefore lose control of open-market operations if there were a difference of opinion within the Committee, if the five nonmembers agreed among themselves, and if only two members of the Board voted with these five. Thus we have the possibility of division within the central management of the Reserve System itself and in regard to the most important power that the System possesses.

While Congress has finally given substantial control of the 12 Federal Reserve banks to the Board of Governors and the Open Market Committee, the individual banks nevertheless retain a significant measure of nuisance power. They decide upon individual applications for rediscounts, they have their own bank examiners, and they can be responsible for delay in determining what the rediscount rate shall be.

The Comptroller of the Currency is the final authority in granting charters for National banks. His agents periodically examine these banks, and by the standards which they enforce they can do much to influence lending policy in the direction of either expansion or contraction. The examiners of the Federal Deposit Insurance Corporation, of the Federal Reserve banks, and of the states, can exercise a similar influence; and they will not necessarily be governed by the same motives.

There are 48 state banking departments, or supervisory agencies of some kind, which are under no obligation to consult with, cooperate with, or give heed to any Federal monetary agency, although there has been in practice some degree of cooperation between state and Federal agencies. Each of the 15,000 banks in the country is a monetary agency in a small way, individually; and collectively they are of major importance.

VI

As part of the desirable changes in the monetary-institutional arrangements in the United States, the volume of business indebtedness should be substantially reduced, although this is by no means indispensable. Short-term obligations in particular give rise to trouble, since they present the opportunity for forced collections in large volume within short periods of time.

The elimination of fractional-reserve banking would be a very desirable element in the reduction of short-term debt, although, again, this is not indispensable. Fractional-reserve banking serves no useful purpose that could not be served equally well in some other manner, and it does have a pernicious influence on the stock of money, although this influence is due in part to a wholly unnecessary legal restriction under which the banks are compelled to operate. This factor will be considered presently. However, under a program of monetary stabilization the chief reason for undesirable variations in the volume of bank loans would be removed, and consequently the banks would offer no insuperable obstacle to the achievement of a high degree of monetary stability. It would be very helpful if reserve ratios were raised to a much higher level than those now prevailing, even though this level were considerably short of 100 per cent.

A higher reserve consisting in part of low-interest-bearing government bonds would be as effective in stabilizing the influence of the banks as would a reserve in the form of either cash or a balance at the Reserve bank. Such bonds should be redeemable at the option of the bank. Balances at the Reserve banks, upon which interest was paid, would not be essentially different from a bond reserve. The objection to a bond reserve is that it would involve the payment of a subsidy to the banks. In the long run and under ideal conditions, there is no reason why those who use the banks for the safekeeping of funds and the clearing of payments should not pay directly for these services.

VII

The unnecessary legal restriction to which reference was made two paragraphs back lies in the fact that, while banks are required to hold only fractional reserves against their deposits, they are not permitted to issue their notes under the same conditions. This is equivalent to 100 per cent reserves for bank notes. I can see no good reason why, if fractional reserves against deposits are desirable, they are not equally to be desired for notes; and yet the defenders of fractional-reserve banking apparently would continue the existing restrictions on bank notes. To be sure, there are fractional reserves against Federal Reserve notes, but this fact does not affect the conditions of operations for member banks. In fact, the prevailing arrangement for the issuance of Federal Reserve notes operates to prevent a complete interconvertibility of notes and deposits. With the current required deposit reserve ratios for the member and Reserve banks, the ultimate required ratio of gold certificates to demand deposits payable to the public is in the neighborhood of 5 per cent (0.25 times approximately 0.20); while the ultimate ratio of certificates to hand-to-hand currency (in the form of Federal Reserve notes) in the hands of the public is 25 per cent.

Any increase in the demand for hand-to-hand currency relative to that for deposits, and a consequent attempt on the part of the public to convert deposits into currency, would deplete the reserves of both the member and the Reserve banks. Without much doubt, this lack of complete interconvertibility between currency and deposits is a very important reason for the perverse behavior of the volume of bank loans. If essentially the present banking structure is retained, the reserve ratio for Federal Reserve notes should be reduced to approximately 5 per cent (or eliminated altogether) to match the ultimate ratio of gold certificates to member-bank deposits payable to the public. An alternative, which the defenders of fractional-reserve banking should propose if they are to be consistent, would be to give to the member banks the privilege of note issue with the same required reserve ratio for notes and deposits.

VIII

The existing monetary-institutional structure of the United States conforms to no one of the points of view enumerated on the first page of this chapter. Those who fear political influence in monetary affairs can point to the manifest willingness of the administrative branch of the government to use its influence in formulating the policy of the Board of Governors, and to the evident inability of the Board to resist this pressure. Those who would have a discretionary authority in control of the monetary system ought logically to ask for the complete centralization of monetary authority, and therefore for the elimination of all those monetary agencies which in some measure, great or small, have the power of nullifying the policy of the Board of Governors. The defenders of an automatic currency system clearly should desire to have fractional-reserve banking eliminated, and this would carry out with it such agencies as the Board of Governors, the Federal Deposit Insurance Corporation, the Comptroller of the Currency, and all the bank-supervisory agencies of the state governments.

It is also evident that a nondiscretionary management of the stock of money requires the concentration of all monetary power delegated by Congress in the hands of a single agency. However, there is no one arrangement for this purpose that is clearly superior to all others. It would be satisfactory if the Secretary of the Treasury were given the necessary authority; but a board of perhaps three members might also be satisfactory. Inasmuch as the criterion of action laid down by Congress might require variations of tax collections, it might also be feasible and desirable to provide for a Congressional Committee to authorize minor changes in tax rates or credits. If such a committee were created, the monetary agent should be responsible to it. Whatever the precise nature of the agency created by Congress, it should be granted the major powers now exercised by the Secretary of the Treasury and by the Board of Governors of the Federal Reserve System.

The monetary agent should acquire the stock of the Federal Reserve banks, and should continue the operation of the existing Reserve banks and their branches in much the same manner as they now function, except that rediscounting should be eliminated if fractional-reserve banking were retained.

The Reserve banks, operating as branches of the monetary agency, should be managed as monetary institutions. In this capacity their most effective weapon is open-market operations. Rediscounting must be upon the initiative of the member bank, whereas all actions designed to influence the stock of money should originate with the monetary agent and be guided by a specific criterion of policy. To be sure, the monetary agency could vary the rediscount rate and thereby in some measure encourage or discourage rediscounting. Nevertheless, even though the response of the banks were prompt, as it would not always be, the effectiveness of this procedure would not equal that of open-market operations. Rediscounting affects only the reserves of the member banks, whereas open-market purchases or sales may vary the size of the cash balances of nonbanking institutions as well as bank reserves. The continuance of the rediscount privilege would be too likely to give the impression that a function of the monetary agency was to assist individual banks in need of additional reserves. The prevalence of this feeling might well give rise to dissatisfaction, criticism, and misunderstanding of the whole program of monetary stabilization if the monetary agency found it necessary to deny petitions for rediscounts in considerable volume. In brief, since rediscount operations provide no positive advantage over the open-market device and they might give rise to some minor difficulty, they should be eliminated.

Chapter 9

THE IMPLEMENTATION OF MONETARY POLICY (Continued)

I

We must now give some attention to the means or devices which may be used in the implementation of monetary policy. More specifically, we must consider the effectiveness and appropriateness of open-market operations and of Federal surpluses and deficits. Can open-market operations be expected to influence aggregate demand directly? Or will their chief influence come by way of their effects on the rate of interest? Will the short- or long-term rate be likely to have the greater influence on investment? May it be necessary to resort to budget surpluses and deficits, either occasionally or consistently? If so, should variations in the budget position be brought about by variations in revenues or in expenditures? If there is to be a constant deficit, should it be achieved by maximizing expenditures or by minimizing revenues?

II

If the criterion of policy were a constant rate of increase in the stock of money, the problem would be simple. As long as there continued to be outstanding Federal indebtedness, the monetary agent should purchase government bonds in the open market to the extent necessary to bring about the desired increase in the stock of money. Funds for these purchases should come from the creation of new money by the monetary agency. Provision should be made for issuance of circulating notes to whatever extent might be necessary to satisfy the desires of the public to divide their cash balances between hand-to-hand currency and deposits. This procedure would progressively raise the reserves of the banks, and consequently, if nothing were done to immobilize these additional reserves, the bond purchases could not equal the annual additions to the stock of money. The gold standard should not be retained, but if it were, accessions to the gold reserves of the monetary system would further reduce the amount of annual bond purchases that could be made with newly created funds.

If the Federal Reserve banks were taken over by the monetary agent, as they should be, it would be immaterial whether their holdings of bonds and those of the Federal agencies and trust funds were redeemed. In May, 1949, all of these holdings were \$57 billion and the total interest-bearing debt was \$250 billion. The remaining \$193 billion of bonds could be extinguished in 22 years if the stock of money were increased at the rate of 3½ per cent a year.[1] To achieve this result, however, the banks could not be permitted to increase their earning assets beyond their present level; the gold standard would have to be abandoned; and Federal tax revenues, including collections under the social security program, would have to equal all Federal payments other than those required for monetizing the debt. This means that interest on the debt would have to be paid out of tax revenues.

Monetization of the debt would afford an excellent opportunity gradually to raise the required reserve ratio of

[1] The quantity of money (hand-to-hand currency plus time and demand deposits, but exclusive of Treasury deposits) was \$166 billion in May, 1949. This \$166 billion, plus the \$193 billion of debt to be redeemed, or \$359 billion, is the amount the stock of money would have to reach to eliminate the debt. 359 is 2.16 times 166, and 1 compounded annually at 3½ per cent will equal 2.13 in 22 years.

the banks. It would only be necessary either to require that an increase in deposits beyond the level prevailing at the time of instituting the program be covered by reserves of 100 per cent, or progressively to raise the reserve requirement against all deposits as the monetization of the debt proceeded. If we again assume that only the $193 billion of debt not held by the Reserve banks or Federal agencies is to be redeemed, and if we also assume that the ratio of deposits to hand-to-hand currency (5.63 to 1) which prevailed in May, 1949, will continue, the increase in deposits resulting from the monetization program would be $164 billion. Since the deposits of all banks in May, 1949, were $141 billion, total deposits would be $305 billion upon completion of the monetization of the debt. If we assume that the reserve requirement against the $141 billion was 15 per cent, or $21 billion, and that reserves of 100 per cent are required against all deposits above $141 billion, the final required reserves against the $305 billion would be $185 billion, or an average ratio of reserves to deposits of 61 per cent.

However, for practical purposes we could substantially eliminate the debt in less than 22 years by immediately putting into effect a bond-reserve requirement, the required reserve ratio being raised sufficiently to absorb the present required reserves, plus the amount of bonds actually held by the banks as of the date of imposition of the new requirement. In May, 1949, the bond holdings of all commercial and mutual savings banks were $74 billion. This amount, plus the existing required reserves of approximately $21 billion, would raise the total required reserves to $95 billion, or 67 per cent of the total deposits of $141 billion.[2]

However, if the reserve requirement were immediately raised to 67 per cent and stabilized at this level, the banks

[2] Manifestly, not all banks would be likely to have the required amount of bonds to meet a requirement of 67 per cent; but it would not be difficult to arrange the transition in such manner as to avoid undue hardships.

would be able to expand their earning assets slightly as the monetization of the nonbank-held debt gave them additional reserves. If we assume that that part of the debt held by the Reserve banks, the Federal agencies, the commercial banks, and the mutual savings banks is not to be redeemed, there will remain only \$119 billion of debt to be monetized. If we again assume that the ratio of deposits to hand-to-hand currency remains at 5.63, the monetization of \$119 billion of debt would give the banks additional deposits of \$101 billion and, of course, an equal addition to their reserves. Of these reserves 67 per cent would be required for the primary deposits which provided them. The excess reserves would therefore be \$33 billion. On the basis of this excess the banks could expand their loans to the extent of approximately \$46 billion, the drain of cash to maintain the ratio of 5.63 to 1 being about \$7 billion.[3]

Upon completion of the monetization of the \$119 billion of debt, the stock of money in billions would be \$331, that is, \$166 + \$119 + \$46. At an annual rate of increase of 3½ per cent, \$166 billion would amount to \$331 billion in 20 years. If a price index were adopted as the criterion of policy, instead of a stable rate of increase in the stock of money, it would be unwise completely to eliminate the bond holdings of nonbankers. The purchase of these bonds in the open market would constitute the quickest means of offsetting a decline in velocity which had brought the index of prices down.

[3] The expansion of \$46 billion is obtained as follows: Let X be the amount of derivative deposits after the drain of cash. The drain of cash will be $X/5.63$. Therefore the cash remaining in the banks after the drain, to serve as reserves for the derivative deposits, will be \$33,-000,000,000 – $(X/5.63)$. These reserves, however, will also be $0.67X$. We therefore have the following equation:

$$33{,}000{,}000{,}000 - \frac{X}{5.63} = 0.67X$$

From this equation we find that X = \$39 billion. The drain of cash is \$7 billion, and therefore the total loan expansion is \$46 billion.

If and when the Federal debt was reduced to the desirable minimum, it would be necessary to find other means of meeting the requirement of a policy of annual additions to the stock of money. Two means only are available: (1) the purchase of other assets than government bonds and (2) the introduction of a permanent deficit in the regular budget. The first of these methods would require the endless accumulation by the government of either commodities or the securities of private corporations. Clearly it must be ruled out.

A balanced budget immediately appeals to one as reasonable and consistent with sound fiscal practices. This feeling is doubtless due in some part to an irrational carrying over of concepts that properly apply only to private business operations; yet it is due in part also to a more or less definite feeling that an unbalanced budget is the means to inflation. Under an automatic gold standard, a balancing of receipts and expenditures would clearly be the proper policy. We cannot, therefore, dismiss the strong feeling in defense of a balanced budget as irrational or "wrong." Nevertheless, there is no good reason why a feeling of attachment to a policy of monetary stabilization might not become as strong, and therefore as much an insurance of sound fiscal practices, as the prevailing attitude toward the gold standard and a balanced budget.

Under a national standard, a secular increase in the quantity of money of as much as 3½ per cent a year would provide for a considerable proportion of governmental expenditures. If the initial quantity of money were $165 billion, the annual increase in the first few years would amount to nearly $6 billion, which would be a substantial proportion of even the highest budget that is likely to prevail. The absolute amount of the annual additions would increase, and so also might the national budget, with increasing national income. Manifestly the proportion of the national expenditures met by the monetary program would change if the rates of increase in the stock of money and in the national budget were not the same.

A given deficit may be produced by an infinite number of levels of expenditure and of tax revenues. We are therefore confronted with this question: Which is preferable, maintenance of expenditures at a high level or holding revenues to a low level? To state the question in this way is virtually to answer it. The requirements of monetary policy are not among the legitimate reasons for undertaking a project which requires an outlay of public funds. Any public expenditure should be based exclusively upon the desirability of the projects for which the expenditures are made. In the implementation of monetary policy, the volume of public outlays should be one of the given data, and the revenues should then be adjusted to this volume in the light of the monetary effects to be achieved.

III

We have been considering the implementation of a monetary policy which required a constant rate of addition to the stock of money. If, instead, our policy were that of stabilizing a price index, the problem of implementation might possibly be more complicated, since it might require either variations in the stock of money or, in a progressive economy, variations in the rate of injection of money. It may be thought that this requirement presents a difficulty. If a marked decline in aggregate demand took place, deficit financing might be more effective in restoring demand than open-market purchases; and yet the latter device would be administratively the simpler. The extent of this difference in effectiveness is problematical; but in any case the question is not of major importance.

Under a policy of stabilization of the price level, monetary action would be taken not so much to bring the index back to "normal" as to confirm the expectations of the public that monetary stability would be maintained. There is a current tendency to look upon a competitive economy as highly unstable. On the contrary, Western industrial economies have shown an impressive degree of stability and resistance to shock in the light of the unstable monetary conditions under which they have been forced to operate throughout their histories. To be sure, we have witnessed marked fluctuations in activity, but we have had no predetermined monetary policy, and even monetary action of the moment has been slow, inadequate, or wanting. If a policy of monetary stability were adopted, we might reasonably expect the spontaneous responses of the system to be sufficient to prevent major difficulties. In other words, required changes in the quantity of money to meet "cyclical" fluctuations in the price level or, in a progressive economy, in the secular rate of injection of money would probably be small in amount. If this position is sound, it follows that the relative effectiveness of open-market operations and deficit or surplus financing is a matter of secondary importance.

While I am convinced that a genuinely competitive economy would maintain a constantly high level of output under conditions of monetary stability, without the necessity of taking action designed directly to influence aggregate demand, there are others who disagree with this position. We should therefore explore the problem of the relative effectiveness of the various devices at our disposal. In a sense I look upon much of the following discussion as irrelevant, since it must be based upon an assumption either of a marked degree of instability in an economy in which a program of monetary stability prevails, or of the prevalence of such monetary instability as would obtain if monetary authority were either diffused or discretionary, or both. These assumptions, however, are clearly those that are tacitly and apparently unconsciously made by a large proportion of present-day writers.

The effect of changes in cash balances on aggregate demand in consequence of open-market operations might conceivably come either indirectly, through changes in the rate of interest, or directly, through an immediate effect on the demand for consumers' or producers' goods.

We should expect the short-term rate of interest to be quite responsive to open-market operations between the banks and the monetary agency, inasmuch as bank reserves would be affected and the banks are an important factor in the short-term loan market. However, it is reasonable to suppose that the demand for short-term loans is highly inelastic, since interest is a relatively insignificant cost to traders. Let us assume that a trader carries an inventory of $120,000, and that his turnover is four per annum. His annual sales would therefore be $600,000 with a markup of 25 per cent. If he borrowed all the funds with which to carry his inventory—an unlikely practice—and the rate were 5 per cent, his interest cost would be $6,000, or 1 per cent of his annual sales.

Now let us assume that an enterprise which requires a heavy investment in fixed equipment and in which there is little use of materials and labor (a hydroelectric plant would be a good example) has an investment of $120,000. Let us assume the rate of depreciation to be 5 per cent, which is equivalent to saying that the annual rate of turnover of the investment is one-twentieth. If all the funds invested in the enterprise were borrowed, again an unlikely practice, and the rate were 5 per cent, the annual interest charge would again be $6,000. The annual sales would have to be 10 per cent of the investment, or $12,000, merely to cover interest and depreciation. Let us assume that the annual cost of materials and labor of all kinds is $12,000, giving annual sales, therefore, of $24,000 if all costs are covered. The interest charge in this case would be 25 per cent of the annual sales.

Admittedly the above figures are only the roughest kind of approximations to reality; and, inasmuch as extreme cases of the two types of investment were deliberately chosen, they may somewhat exaggerate the difference in the relative importance of interest charges to traders and to investors in fixed capital. Nevertheless, they do show the relative insignificance of interest on short-term loans to enterprises with a high rate of turnover; and they make inevitable the conclusion, not only that the demand for such loans is very inelastic, but that it is much more so than is the demand for long-term loans.

However, we have ignored one factor which would tend to produce elasticity in the short-term demand to some uncertain but probably slight extent. There must be some fringe of borrowing which enterprisers are willing to do in either the long- or the short-term market, depending upon the relative rates of interest on the two types of loans. If, for example, the short-term rate went down, while the long-term rate did not, there would presumably be not only some additional borrowing on short-term at the expense of long-term loans at the prevailing long-term rate, but some additional borrowing on short-term that would have been done in the long-term market had the long-term rate gone down. In the event, therefore, that the long-term rate did not change at all, a decline in the short-term rate would somewhat increase the total amount of borrowing through this shifting operation; while if the long-term rate went down, but only some time after the short-term rate, the effect of the shift between the markets would be to hasten the response of borrowers to the open-market operations. Nevertheless, it seems unlikely that changes in the short-term rate would produce much change in the amount of funds demanded, and we would be unjustified, therefore, in anticipating much effect from these changes.

There is a further objection to an attempt to implement monetary policy by means of variations in short-term bank lending. Debt financing is an unfortunate element in modern business practices, and the bankers are likely to encourage the more perverse aspect of this practice, since their desire for both liquid and income-yielding assets may well induce borrowers to resort in greater measure than otherwise they would to short-term financing. The prevalence of large volumes of maturities and near maturities is an exceedingly disturbing factor to business firms at a time when lenders become reluctant to risk their funds; and the greater the proportion of short-term debt, the greater the volume of maturities within a given period of time. To base a program of monetary control, either in whole or in part, on the requirement of variations in the debt holdings of the banks will lead to the continuance and encouragement of a form of financing which itself tends to accentuate the influence of destabilizing factors. Such a program, therefore, contains a very large element of internal inconsistency.

The effect of open-market operations on the long-term rate of interest is uncertain. An isolated open-market purchase of government bonds by a monetary agency, in the absence of an established monetary policy, "ought" to cause corporation bond prices to fall and share prices to rise, since it would be evidence of an intention on the part of the monetary agency to raise commodity prices. This rise in the general price level would raise the market rate of interest and increase the monetary earnings of equities in industrial corporations. The shift in relative prices of bonds and shares could readily be brought about through the purchase of shares by sellers of government bonds and through a shift of their investments from bonds to shares by holders of corporation bonds. The (temporary) effect would be a rise in the prices of government bonds, a fall in the prices of corporation bonds, and a rise in the prices of shares.

Nevertheless, it is by no means certain that the market would react in the short run to an open-market purchase in the above manner. In the first place, in the absence of an announced policy of monetary stabilization there would be much uncertainty as to the extent of the expected rise in commodity prices, and the promised increase of returns on shares at their current prices might therefore be insufficient to overcome established practices of investors in regard to their relative holdings of bonds and shares. It is conceivable, therefore, that nonbanking sellers of government bonds might reinvest their funds in corporation bonds and thus create pressure for a rise, instead of a fall, in the prices of these bonds. In the second place, to the extent that banks were sellers to the monetary agency, the result would almost certainly be in the direction of rising corporation bond prices, since the banks do not purchase shares. It is clear, therefore, that even though nonbanking investors shifted to shares, the influence of the banks might prevent a decline in the prices of corporation bonds.

If the open-market purchase were in pursuance of an established policy of monetary stabilization, there would be a greater likelihood that corporation-bond prices would rise. In fact, it is unlikely that they would fail to rise. The knowledge of the public that no substantial changes in commodity prices were to be encountered would lead investors to anticipate no significant changes in the money earnings on shares; and since it was bonds they had sold, they would be likely to reinvest in corporation bonds the cash received from the sale of government bonds. This tendency would be reenforced by the action of the banks. The probable effect, therefore, of the open-market purchase would be a (temporary) rise in the price of both government and corporation bonds and no change in the prices of shares.

While it is probable that the demand for long-term loans has a considerable measure of elasticity, it is less probable that investment (in the Keynesian sense) would respond immediately to a change in the long-term rate. Men will require time to ponder over the possible advantages of a decrease in the rate of interest and to make definite decisions concerning new construction projects. It will take further time to make engineering plans and to let the necessary contracts for materials and construction work. On the other hand, many firms are undoubtedly more or less continuously considering possibilities of additional investment and therefore have available in various stages of development plans for capital outlays. Where this is true, a reduction in the rate of interest might frequently be an impelling reason for putting some of these plans into effect. In such cases, therefore, the reaction to open-market purchases would be prompt. However, if it were necessary to rely wholly upon the positive effects of open-market operations, rather than upon an inherent tendency of the system toward stability under an established and definite monetary policy, the slowness of response to open-market purchases and sales might lead to somewhat greater fluctuations in prices and output than would be encountered if aggregate demand could be immediately affected. Nevertheless, even though the economy exhibited a less degree of stability than I should expect, open-market operations in pursuance of an announced monetary policy would undoubtedly prevent such severe fluctuations in prices and output as we have known in the past; partly because of the effect, even though somewhat delayed, on the rate of investment, but to a greater extent because of the stability of expectations which they would engender.

It is unlikely that there would be much, if any, immediate effect on aggregate demand in consequence of open-market operations. Since the sellers, or buyers, of the government bonds would be preponderantly banks and institutional investors, the cash balances of consumers and of business firms would not be much affected immediately. However, there might be some delayed influence on consumers' demand quite independently of any rise in income in consequence of an increase in investment. If and as bond prices rose, the rising value of their bond holdings might induce individual bondholders to spend more liberally. Nevertheless, it seems doubtful that we should be warranted in placing much reliance upon open-market operations as a means of directly influencing aggregate demand through the demand for consumers' goods.

If the maximum effect from open-market operations is to be realized, the government must restrict its outstanding interest-bearing obligations to instruments which carry neither a requirement nor an option on the part of the government to redeem at stipulated values, but which must be purchased at the market price if they are to be retired. These are consols. The issuance of fixed-maturity obligations by the Federal government tends to obscure the monetary significance of Treasury operations. Government debt serves well the purpose of money in the "cash" reserves of the public, since it can certainly be converted into actual cash on short notice. The shorter the maturity, the less is the possible fluctuation in price and hence the better will the instrument serve as a substitute for money.

The present practice of issuing obligations with a wide range of maturities from demand to many years inevitably results in confusion on the part of all concerned—the Secretary of the Treasury, Congress, the general public, and Professor Hansen! The Series E bonds well illustrate the state of confusion on this question. They are redeemable on short notice at the option of the holder, and they bear a relatively high rate of interest. They should, therefore, be attractive to investors. Furthermore, they may not be purchased by banks, and therefore their sale cannot lead directly to an expansion of bank credit. On the basis of these facts, the Series E bonds seem admirably adapted to noninflationary financing of the government. But they are excellent substitutes for cash in the "cash" balances of the public, and consequently when they are bought the buyer obtains something which serves almost as well the purposes of money as the money he pays for them. The result must be that the sale of Series E bonds operates in some unknown measure to raise velocity, and this is quite as effective in raising prices as an increase in the quantity of money.

Hansen has demurred to the proposal that the government restrict itself to the issuance of consols and money, eschewing the use of short-term, interest-bearing obligations. In this connection he makes the following statement: [4]

> The rate of interest will be determined in large degree by the relative use made of (1) the multiplication of money or (2) borrowing from the public. Having decided upon an appropriate level of interest rates, however, various combinations of (1) public spending, (2) tax revenues, (3) borrowing from the public, and (4) multiplication of money can be applied to produce full employment at substantially stable prices.

Even on the basis of Hansen's contention that the control of the rate of interest should be the immediate consideration in monetary policy, and that the rate (not the price level) will be influenced by a change in the quantity of money, he should agree that only consols and money should be issued; and the issuance of consols should be only for the purpose of decreasing the quantity of money, never for the purpose of financing a deficit which, as he would say, is itself needed to maintain employment. Why should he want to borrow from the nonbanking public? Supposedly for the purpose of withdrawing money and raising the rate of interest; but if so, consols would be better than short-term instruments, since they would be less like money than the short-term obligations. If monetary policy calls for an increase in the quantity of money, Hansen would borrow from the banks to an extent for which he gives no criterion. Why? To subsidize the banks in order that they may avoid service charges! I see no reason why writers of checks

[4] Alvin H. Hansen, *Economic Policy and Full Employment* (McGraw-Hill Book Company, Inc., 1947), p. 215.

should be granted such favored treatment. Hansen confuses the issue of the means of bringing about needed variations in the stock of money by introducing wholly unrelated problems in defense of his position. Granted that we did want to subsidize the banks, the requirements of monetary policy should not be subordinated to this desire.

Short-term obligations are attractive to our misguided secretaries of the Treasury because they permit low rates on governmental borrowing. The interest charges of the government should be minimized, but by minimizing borrowing, not by low rates that are incompatible with a sensible monetary policy. When fulfillment of a commitment to take monetary action under given conditions requires an increase in the quantity of money, it is preposterous to borrow from the banks. Borrowing should be resorted to only as a means of withdrawing money from circulation for the purpose of avoiding inflation; and lending should be equally restricted to the single purpose of preventing deflation. If the government debt is to be managed in this manner, it is clear that borrowing should be on the basis of obligations that are least like money. These are consols.

The higher interest charges on consols would be a small price to pay for monetary stability. However, aggregate interest charges would not, in fact, be high, since in an expanding economy borrowing to prevent inflation would in the long run be more than offset by lending to avoid deflation. Even in a stationary economy, borrowing to maintain monetary stability could never be for more than small amounts and at infrequent intervals.

A deficit or surplus in the Federal budget can be produced by a change either in expenditures or in tax revenues. Precisely why there is currently so strong a feeling in favor of variation of expenditures is not clear, although it is probably compounded of at least four different factors: (1) Those who stress the importance of investment in maintaining employment quite naturally turn to public investment, either as a permanent or an intermittent adjunct to private investment. (2) There seems to be a feeling that only if public moneys are paid out for "worth-while" projects do we "get something for our money" if a deficit is incurred. (3) Many economists hold that deficit financing will be more effective if it requires direct income payments to wage earners, rather than reductions of the amounts collected from taxpayers. (4) Finally, I suspect that many supporters of a public-works program seize upon this as an aid in securing the particular kind of redistribution of income that they desire.

Even though it should be true that an increased propensity to hoard is in the first instance chiefly at the expense of investment, it does not necessarily follow that the only or the best remedy is to attempt, more or less directly, to maintain investment by means of public works. The real difficulty is variations in the demand for cash. Its impact on investment is a secondary and incidental matter. Current discussions that stress the problem of investment are not utterly wrong in all the details of their analyses; but they are grossly misleading in the emphasis they place upon the supposed need for a direct support of investment. The required action is that of changing the stock of money in response to changes in the demand for cash. If this is done, the needed maintenance of aggregate demand will be secured, and it makes little difference whether the effect is manifested chiefly in the markets for producers' or consumers' goods. Indeed, it is my thesis that if a policy of monetary stabilization prevails there will be no occasion for combatting a serious decline in aggregate demand.

I may be setting up a straw man in suggesting that some defenders of public works feel that only in this way shall we "get something for our money" in deficit spending, since I know of no writer who has said precisely this. Casual statements, however, give this impression. In any case, the answer is simple. If a deficit is created by reducing revenues, the expenditures of the government are presumably as "useful" as they would be were expenditures increased. Any difference in this respect between the two procedures, therefore, depends upon the relative "usefulness" of the expanded private expenditures, in consequence of reduced taxes, and upon the alternative of expanded public expenditures. If one defends freedom of choice for the individual, the conclusion must be that the private expenditures will in fact be the more "useful." A contrary conclusion rejects the foundation itself of a free society. Manifestly, the relevant question is that of the relative effectiveness in maintaining output of expanded public expenditures and the expanded private disposable incomes that result from tax reduction.

Those who propose a variable volume of public expenditures seek some device that will directly and immediately affect aggregate demand. They hold, in effect, that the essential task of monetary-fiscal policy is that of reducing the extent of unavoidable booms and deep depressions. They imply that a competitive economy, even though it operates under conditions of monetary stability, is so highly unstable that it will not continuously maintain a high level of output. They constantly refer to conditions of extreme depression and assert that under those conditions the propensity to hoard is so highly elastic that virtually unlimited quantities of money may be added to the system without appreciable effect on aggregate demand. In this vein, Hansen declares that "it requires long planning ahead to be prepared to meet a head-on depression. . . . Yet we know, as certainly as we know anything, that in a few years this problem will be upon us."[5] To be sure, one must agree with Hansen if no adequate policy of monetary stabilization is instituted; but the implication of his statement is that the problem, in any event, is that of meeting

[5] *Ibid.*, p. vii.

a "head-on" depression, not of adopting a policy that will maintain a reasonable approach to stability at all times.

Such problems as public works or public expenditures for other purposes, redistribution of income, and monetary policy are unrelated in their major aspects, and each is of sufficient importance to stand on its own merits. We shall never arrive at reasonable decisions in regard to these questions until each is so considered. No economist has done more to confuse the issues by failing to distinguish between the problems of monetary policy and of public expenditures for welfare purposes than has Hansen. Note the following statements, which come in the midst of a consideration of monetary policy: [6]

> Consider the wholly inadequate educational facilities in the southern and other backward states which include about 40 per cent of American children, and the grave deficiency in public health facilities as revealed by the military draft.
>
> For myself I am convinced that a study of the serious deficiencies in this country will indicate that large public outlays are necessary. They are necessary in areas where private enterprise cannot enter.

I would not disagree with Hansen on the need for greater expenditures on education. I ask only that consideration of expenditures for welfare purposes be dissociated from the discussion of monetary policy and that, once expenditures for a given purpose are decided upon, they be stabilized. Would Hansen reduce expenditures for education and public health if the price level rose? Of course, he would not. Why, then, does he bring such considerations into a discussion of monetary policy? Apparently he does so because of his persistent failure to distinguish among three unrelated problems in which he is interested: (1) He believes that *variable* expenditures are

[6] "Notes on Mints' Paper on Monetary Policy," *Review of Economic Statistics,* XXVIII (Harvard University Press, 1946), 70.

required to reduce the extent of fluctuations in employment; (2) he wants a generally *high* level of public expenditures to avoid a chronically low level of employment, which he thinks will otherwise prevail; and (3) he would like to see an expansion of public expenditures in certain directions for purely welfare purposes. He unconsciously, and of course without warning, wanders back and forth among these distinct problems and muddies the water completely.

If public works, of whatever kind they may be, are desirable in themselves, they should not be required to wait upon the development of undesirable monetary conditions. Moreover, despite the lamentations of Keynes, Hansen, and others, we are still living in an economy of scarcity, and it therefore behooves us to consider carefully the relative importance of all the various competing demands upon our limited resources and to use those resources with the utmost economy. The danger is great that a project undertaken primarily for the purpose of implementing monetary policy will not represent the most desirable utilization of resources. Moreover, if the "wrong" decision were made, the wastage of resources would certainly be greater than would be the case if the decision were that of a business firm, since in the latter case the losses incurred would sharply limit the flow of resources in an undesired direction. The continuous check of profits and losses in private enterprise is largely absent in public undertakings. No community is so wealthy that it can afford to overlook this fact.

Quite aside from the above considerations, there are positive objections to public works as a means of implementing monetary policy. While the need for promptness of action can be overemphasized, action without undue delay is nevertheless desirable. To minimize the lag in action, it is currently demanded that public works be planned in advance, thus making it possible, so it is said, to institute construction work in a very short time. Planning would be of some help, but its merits are vastly overrated. With the best of planning, time would be lost before an increase of expenditures would be possible. Either discontinuance of deficit spending would have to take place too gradually for monetary purposes, or construction projects would have to be left incomplete until same later need for monetary action arose.

The use of plans made any considerable length of time in advance would almost certainly involve a waste of resources. Changes in technology, shifts in population, the rise and fall of industries and geographic areas, would render many plans obsolete within a few years. This fact would be so evident that in numerous instances plans would be thoroughly revised before they were acted upon.

A more cumbersome and unsuitable means of achieving monetary stability than that of variations in public works would be difficult to invent. It would be slow, wasteful, and less effective than alternative devices.

What would be the probable effect of variations in tax revenues, expenditures being constant, in an economy which was markedly unstable, despite a policy of monetary stabilization? Let us consider the case of a decrease in tax rates while employment is declining, the deficit thus produced being met by the issuance of new money. The increase in the stock of money would both raise the real value of all assets held by the public and change the relative holdings of cash and other assets, since the value of other assets would be unchanged and that of cash increased until the additions to the stock of money became effective in raising prices. The real value of cash would be further increased, and that of other assets would not be decreased, by the decline in the price level which would accompany (and in part cause) the decline in employment. The relative quantities of various assets held can hardly be a matter of pure chance, and if it is not, the additions to the stock of money would quickly increase the demand for both producers' and consumers' goods. Furthermore, the effect on aggregate demand of the increase in cash balances would be reenforced by the increase in disposable income resulting from the tax reduction. Without reasonable doubt, a reduction of tax rates or exemption levels, or an increase in tax credits under the income tax, would be effective in raising aggregate demand.

The question remains as to the speed with which changes in tax rates might be obtained. If Congressional action were required, there would necessarily be some delay, although if Congress could once be convinced of the need for prompt action in regard to this matter the lag in action would not be unduly great. Possibly some limited discretionary power to vary tax rates, exemption levels, or tax credits could be granted to an administrative official or to a joint Congressional committee to which the administrative official in charge of monetary action would be responsible. There would, however, be some delay in changing collections after the action in regard to rates had been taken, even for that part of taxes collected currently. It seems evident that variation of tax rates would be much less than an ideal means of changing the quantity of money, and yet it could probably be used with a fair degree of success.

Our conclusion with respect to the relative merits of tax and expenditure variations must clearly rest upon our answer to these three questions: (1) What will be their relative effectiveness in maintaining aggregate demand? (2) Which will give the more prompt effect? (3) Which will restrict individual freedom of choice less? If the conclusions reached in the preceding discussion are valid, there would be no significant difference in the effectiveness of the two devices in maintaining aggregate demand. While both methods would involve some delay in action, there can be no reasonable doubt that this delay would be greater with the use of variable expenditures. Anyone who has an interest in individual freedom must answer the third question emphatically in favor of variable taxes. While our final conclusion, therefore, must be that variable taxes are preferable to variable expenditures, nevertheless, neither device would be ideal in implementing a policy of monetary stabilization.

However, the problem is not that of combatting a developed depression or inflationary boom. A competitive, free-enterprise economy requires for stable functioning certain general rules in accordance with which businessmen can make confident calculations and contracts. An essential rule of this kind is that of a firm commitment on the part of the state to take monetary action in accordance with a specific and unambiguous criterion. To meet the requirement for short-period *variations* in the stock of money under such a rule, open-market operations would probably be adequate. Secular changes in the stock of money, however, would have to be provided for in the budget after the national debt had been reduced to a reasonable minimum. For this purpose, changes in tax rates would not have to be made with undue frequency.

IV

A policy of increasing the quantity of money at some constant rate, of stabilizing a price-level index, and of stabilizing the Federal budget in the manner suggested by Friedman would not work out so differently in practice as one might at first suppose. Manifestly, after the Federal debt was eliminated and provided that 100 per cent reserve banking were introduced, a policy of annually increasing the stock of money, under a national monetary system, would require a deficit equal to the desired increase in the quantity of money and constantly rising at a stable rate. Open-market operations would be required, however, to maintain the rate of increase during the year if for any reason the budget estimates were not realized. If fractional-reserve banking were retained, the computation of the required budget deficit would be more complicated and the needed deficit itself would be both smaller and less likely to provide precisely for the desired increase. If we let *B* equal the amount of the required budget deficit; r, the reserve ratio of the banks; D, the amount of the increase in the stock of money that will be made up of deposits; and H, the amount of increase in the form of hand-to-hand currency, we have the following equation:

$$B = rD + H$$

Either D or H alone might be negative, depending upon the desires of the public as to their relative holdings of hand-to-hand currency and deposits. A negative value, however, would be improbable, particularly for D. If, for example, the increase in the stock of money were to be 1,000, and of this the public desired 800 and 200 in the form of deposits and hand-to-hand currency, respectively; and if, further, the reserve ratio of the banks were 25 per cent, the required budget deficit would be 400. It is evident that the deficit of 400 would not be realized if revenues or expenditures were not as predicted, and the 400 would itself be incorrect if the public changed their relative holdings of deposits and hand-to-hand currency during the year, or if the banks failed to maintain the maximum amount of deposits permitted by their reserves.

Since failure of the deficit to be of the right amount might require interim open-market operations, it would be desirable to maintain some minimum amount of Federal indebtedness. This amount would vary with purchases and sales by the monetary agency, and with deficits of unanticipated amounts; but if it showed a persistent tendency to fall, the budget would have to be adjusted in such manner as to bring it back to the desired minimum. If the problem were that of combatting an actual deflation or inflation of some magnitude, a relatively small amount of outstanding government obligations would be very desirable, since in an essentially unstable economy it would be the purpose of the open-market operations to influence (temporarily) the rate of interest and thereby aggregate demand. If the outstanding volume of securities were small, purchases and sales in relatively small amounts would have pronounced effects on the rate of interest.

However, if it be true that the economy would autonomously maintain a high average level of employment under a reasonable rule of monetary action, the effect on the rate of interest becomes a matter of secondary importance. Furthermore, if fractional-reserve banking were eliminated, the extent to which the deficit might fail to provide for the desired increase in the stock of money would be greatly reduced. Under these circumstances it is possible that the inherent stability of the system would be such that a deficit of an improper amount within the year would produce no untoward effect, with the result that open-market operations could be avoided, compensatory action being postponed until the budget for the following year was made up.

If the policy adopted were that of stabilizing an index of the price level, short-term changes in the stock of money might be required, and certainly a secular increase would be necessary in an expanding economy. After the reduction of the national debt to the desired minimum, and provided that fractional-reserve banking were eliminated, this policy would require that the annual budget provide for a deficit equal to the estimated addition to the stock of money that would be needed to maintain stability in the price level. If the commercial banks were retained, a smaller deficit would be required. In both cases the amounts would be substantially the same as the annual deficits that would be required with the same conditions under a policy of increasing the stock of money at a constant rate. In so far, therefore, as the secular problem is concerned, there would be no difference in the manner of implementing these two policies.

If within the year the index reached either the upper or the lower limit of tolerance, open-market operations would be required. It is highly probable that the stability of the economy would be such that these operations would be adequate to bring the index back to "normal," in which case no "cyclical" changes in tax rates would ever become necessary. If open-market operations proved not to be adequate, money income would rise or fall, with consequent increases or decreases in revenues, with constant tax rates, precisely similar to those that would emerge under the Friedman stable-budget plan. Since the annual budgets would provide for a secular increase in the stock of money, it is at least possible that no "cyclical" open-market operations would ever be needed. In any case, it is clear that there would in practice be little difference between a policy of increasing the quantity of money at a stable rate and of stabilizing an index of the price level.

Under the Friedman budget plan, "cyclical" surpluses and deficits would result from rising and falling incomes, respectively. The secular effects on the price level would depend upon the nature of the expenditures that were stabilized, whether real or money, aggregate or per capita, and upon the cause of the expansion of the economy, whether increasing population or advancing technology. Table 10 indicates the various possibilities for stabilizing expenditures, and the secular effect of each on the price level.

We can perhaps discover most easily a first approximation to the effect on the price level by assuming stability of prices. In an expanding economy an increase in the stock of money would be required for this effect, although an unchanging quantity of money would provide for stability of wage rates but not of product prices, if population were stable and technology were advancing. If with our assumption of stability of prices the effect on the budget is not such as to bring about an increase in the quantity of money, it is evident that this assumption is incompatible with the effects of the policy. So long as we retain the assumption of stable prices, cases 1 and 2 are the same. So also are cases 3 and 4, and 5 to 8 inclusive.

TABLE 10. SECULAR EFFECT ON THE PRICE LEVEL OF THE FRIEDMAN STABLE-BUDGET PLAN

	Cause of expansion of the economy		Basis of stabilization of expenditures				Effect on the price level
	Growth of population	Advancing technology	Per capita		Aggregate		
			Real	Money	Real	Money	
1	x		x				Deflation, including wages
2	x			x			Deflation, including wages
3	x				x		Deflation, including wages
4	x					x	Deflation, including wages
5		x	x				Deflation, including wages
6		x		x			Deflation, not including wages
7		x			x		Deflation, including wages
8		x				x	Deflation, not including wages

In case 1—that of a growing population and stable per capita real expenditures—revenues would rise with stable prices, equally with population, but so also would expenditures. Consequently no deficit would appear, and there would be no addition to the stock of money. Manifestly, prices could not in fact be stable. They would decline, and wage rates would be included in the decline. Money expenditures per capita would fall, but the growth in population would substantially offset this, so that aggregate expenditures should be little changed, if at all. On the other hand, revenue clearly would decline. Were the income tax not progressive, the decline in revenue per capita would be offset by the growth in the number of taxpayers; but with a progressive tax and a constantly declining per capita money income, total revenue would fall. A deficit would result, but it could not be sufficient to prevent the fall in prices since the deficit itself would be the consequence of the decline in prices and incomes.

The same assumption of stable per capita real expenditures, but with a stable population and advancing technology (case 5) yields much the same result. If prices are provisionally held to be constant, both expenditures and revenues will be unchanged and, consequently, no deficit will appear to provide for the increase in the stock of money necessary to support stability of prices. Stable prices are again incompatible with the policy adopted. It may at first appear that the quantity of money will be unchanged and that, consequently, wage rates will be constant while commodity prices will fall. This, however, is not the case. As commodity prices fell, a surplus would appear, unless wage rates (incomes) also fell, but wage rates would not fall until after the surplus had appeared. Consequently there would be a persistent tendency for a surplus to develop and for the quantity of money to decline. To be sure, as wage rates declined revenues would fall, but this development could not prevent the appearance of a surplus, since it would be the surplus that would produce the decrease in incomes. The secular drag on wage rates might be quite as severe as in the case of a growing population and stable per capita real expenditures.

If the policy adopted were that of maintaining constancy in per capita *money* expenditures (cases 2 and 6), we again find that no deficit would appear, with the provisional assumption of stable prices and that, consequently, prices would necessarily fall. However, with a growing population money expenditures would rise, despite the fall proportionately with population in prices, as they would not with any of the other policies, and therefore a given decline in money incomes would produce a greater deficit than would any alternative policy. This policy, therefore, would be the least deflationary of all with a growing population. With a stable population and advancing technology, again no deficit would appear under the provisional assumption of stable prices. However, this would also be true even though product prices fell if wage rates did not. Since equilibrium would require a decline in product prices relative to wage rates, it is evident that this policy is compatible with wage stability, but not with stability of product prices. There can be no objection to a policy which has this effect, but unfortunately if, in addition to advancing technology, population were growing, stable per capita money expenditures would produce a constant drag on wage rates. Nevertheless, this is the best result that can be obtained under the stable-budget plan.

How serious would be the consequences of a constant downward pressure on wage rates cannot be predicted. In large part the effects would be dependent upon the degree of flexibility of wage rates, and this is itself an uncertain matter. In practice the rate of decline in wage rates under the stable-budget plan could not be so great as the rate of growth of population, since this rate would be reached only if the quantity of money were constant, whereas in actuality there would be *some* increase in the stock of money in consequence of the budget deficit that would appear with declining money incomes. Probably, therefore, the required rate of decline in rates of pay could not be so much as 1 per cent per annum. This seems small, and yet it is probably more the requirement of a decrease than the amount of this decrease that is of importance. Persons with fixed incomes might gain, and those with flexible incomes would not lose in real terms. Creditors would gain, and debtors would lose, both in considerable amounts in the course of a generation, unless the rate of interest were adjusted downward in anticipation of the decline in the price level.

Since the effects of the policy on the price level would be definite and predictable, a generally lower level of interest rates would in fact probably prevail. However, no adjustment of the interest rate would be possible that would completely eliminate gains and losses.[7] If rates were lower, annuitants would not gain from the rising value of money, since the amount of annuity that could be purchased with a given premium would be less than could have been secured at higher rates of interest. However, even though gradually declining wage rates had no serious consequences, there would be no positive advantage to be derived from such a requirement; and therefore, since there is a high probability of adverse effects, discretion alone would suggest that we should avoid this necessity if at all possible.

The automatic anti-"cyclical" features of the stable-budget plan could be retained if the budget were "balanced" in such manner as to provide for a secular growth in the stock of money equal to the rate of growth of population. If this were done, however, annual changes in either the tax structure or expenditures would be required. This necessity would very much reduce the attractiveness of the plan, since its chief recommendation consists of its automatic operation; and yet either increasing the stock of money at a constant rate or stabilizing an index of the price level would likewise require annual legislation to provide for the necessary and constantly rising deficit. However, it is important to note that a deficit required for this reason would make possible the development of reasonable criteria for budget making. The amount of the deficit required for monetary purposes and the level of expenditures for welfare reasons could then be, and should be, determined completely independently of each other. It would then be clear that any expenditures in excess of the needed increase in the stock of money should be covered by taxes.

[7] On this point see C. M. Walsh, "The Steadily Appreciating Standard," *Quarterly Journal of Economics,* XI (1896–1897), 280–295.

The preceding discussion of implementation makes it clear that a policy of increasing the quantity of money at a constant rate might require open-market operations within the tax year, particularly if fractional-reserve banking were retained; a policy of stabilizing a price index would be somewhat more likely to require such operations, although, even in this case, they might be avoided; and the stable-budget plan would, of course, prohibit these operations. All three policies would require a budget deficit (after reduction of the public debt to some desirable minimum) as a means of providing for an annual increase in the quantity of money, if we desired—as we should—to avoid a secular drag on wage rates. Moreover, since the rate of increase in the stock of money should be stable, the actual amount of yearly increase should constantly rise. This rising amount would necessitate annual legislation in regard to tax rates or expenditures.

Both the deficit and the annual changes in either tax rates or expenditures would be unfortunate. In the end the greatest sin of the Keynesians may well prove to have been the encouragement of the belief on the part of taxpayers that public expenditures can be costless to themselves. It is currently insisted by many persons that an enlargement of public expenditures, to be financed wholly or in part by means of a deficit which is met by the creation of new money, is not only costless in the sense that taxes are in some measure unnecessary, but that it will be of outright benefit to the community in that chronic unemployment will otherwise prevail. This attitude must surely have dulled the sensitivity of taxpayers to an expansion of public expenditures. The consequences, at the very least, are likely to be an "uneconomic" allocation of resources as the result of an irresponsible and unnecessary extension of public activities. At the worst, we may be destined for an experience with inflation which no one wants.

However, if once the need for monetary stability were recognized, it is not too much to hope that canons of "respectability" in regard to budgetary practices could be established which would promote responsibility in legislative appropriations. Under these circumstances the amount of deficit needed for monetary purposes would be the starting point in making up the budget. It should then be recognized that any extension of public expenditures beyond this amount should invariably be covered dollar for dollar by tax receipts, and that every item of expenditure should stand on its merits, without regard to the problem of monetary policy. If these criteria of budget policy were adopted, a deficit and annual legislation would not lead to undesirable consequences.

V

In the light of all the relevant considerations, both of the promise of success in maintaining stability and of the difficulties of implementation, it appears that there are at least four monetary policies that would be reasonably satisfactory. They are, in the reverse of their order of probable desirability, (1) a genuinely automatic international gold standard, (2) the stable-budget plan, (3) a constant rate of increase in the stock of money, and (4) stabilization of the price level.

An automatic gold standard has little to recommend it if it is not international, and it clearly will not yield satisfactory results in association with fractional-reserve banking. Given the proper conditions for its functioning, however, a gold standard would afford the basis for fairly confident forecasts of the stock of money for a sufficient number of years in advance to provide a high degree of monetary stability. The annual additions to the quantity of money, even though not in the most desirable amounts, would not be likely either to bring on inflation or to constitute a substantial drag on wage rates. Its very great merits would arise from the elimination of all discretionary and legislative action, except for the initial determination of the quantity of gold in the monetary unit, and from the possibility of a balanced budget at all times. However, in the unlikely event that fluctuations in the level of output were of considerable magnitude, a gold standard would offer little possibility of either a deliberately managed or an automatic corrective response of the monetary system, since open-market operations would be inappropriate, and the budget should be balanced at all times. There would be some compensatory response through the reaction of changes in the price level upon the output of the mines, but this would be too slow and small in amount to be significant in the short run, although it would limit the extent of secular changes in the price level. A somewhat greater anti-"cyclical" effect could be expected from the change in the value of cash balances as the price level rose or fell.

A gold standard requires the use of resources in mining which might better be employed in other occupations if the monetary system can be made to operate successfully without reliance on gold. It may be thought that the volume of such resources could be reduced by including in the stock of money either a fixed or a constantly increasing amount of fiduciary money, but on examination this saving proves to be largely illusory. Let us suppose that a fixed fiduciary issue is introduced. Initially prices and costs would be higher than otherwise they would have been. This fact would in the short run reduce the amount of resources used in mining and the output of gold, and it would increase the consumption of gold by industry. But the smaller output and increased industrial consumption would mean that prices would constantly decline more rapidly than they would have without the fiduciary issue. This tendency would continue until the value of gold was precisely the same as it would have been under a nonfractional-reserve gold standard. From then on the output of gold would also be the same in the two cases, and consequently thereafter no saving of resources would be realized from the fiduciary issue. By means of a constant additional injection of fiduciary currency some saving of resources could be had, since this would continuously postpone the completion of the adjustment. But in this case a constant budget deficit would be required, and consequently we would then have eliminated a balanced budget and the completely automatic operation of the system, two of the more important of its advantages.[8]

The stable-budget plan would again give little promise of success if fractional-reserve banking were retained, since there is no reason to suppose that the deficits and surpluses of the budget would offset the perverse creation and extinction of bank money. In the absence of the banks, however, the automatic compensatory reactions of the budget would be of significant magnitude in meeting fluctuations in output. The advantage of the plan lies in this nondiscretionary character of its anti-"cyclical" action. Nevertheless, there is no assurance that the automatic changes in revenues would be more nearly of the "right" amount than would the open-market operations of a stable-price-level policy. Unfortunately, with a growing population, the stable-budget policy would require a continuing deficit and annual legislation on tax rates or expenditures if a secular drag on wage rates was to be avoided. It is also doubtful that the relationship of a stable budget to monetary stability would be so clear to the public as would that of a policy of stabilizing a price index. If not, the reaction of the business community would not be so likely by itself to maintain equilibrium, and the need for positive compensatory action would therefore be greater.

A policy of steadily increasing the stock of money at a rate roughly equivalent to the rate of increase in transactions would probably yield very satisfactory results. Its

[8] The analysis of this paragraph is based upon an unpublished manuscript by Mr. Homer Jones. His paper is not available to me at the present time, and what I have written may possibly not agree with his analysis in all respects.

chief merits lie in its simplicity and preciseness. Moreover, it could be operated with the retention of fractional-reserve banking, although it would function in a better manner, as would any policy, if the banks were eliminated. A possible drawback would arise from the absence of "cyclical" compensatory reactions of the monetary system, either automatic or deliberate. How important this would be cannot be foretold. My guess is that it would prove to be a minor matter. A further drawback would arise from any perverse contraction or expansion of the stock of money by the banks, since such developments might require short-term open-market operations. The needed amount of purchases or sales would be as uncertain as under a policy of stabilizing a price index, inasmuch as it would be impossible to foretell precisely the extent to which the banks would respond, in the short run, to the change in their reserves. However, perverse action by the banks would be rendered much less likely than now by the policy itself. A secularly increasing quantity of money would require a continuing deficit, after the reduction of the national debt to reasonable proportions, and this fact would necessitate annual legislation in regard to either taxes or expenditures.

In my judgment a policy of stabilizing a price index as heavily weighted with the prices of domestic commodities as was practically possible would give best results, although the margin of superiority might in practice prove to be small. Admittedly this opinion rests in part upon an appraisal of the importance of a number of imponderables. The promised advantages of this policy lie in the fact that it corresponds to the most understandable meaning of the concept of monetary stability, and it affords the opportunity for prompt and ample action to offset disturbances. However, from this latter fact also arises a possible drawback. Of necessity, discretionary control over the extent of open-market operations would be given to the monetary agency, and the lag in effect might conceivably cause an unwanted magnification of autonomous developments, although what evidence we have suggests the contrary, rather than an offsetting of tendencies in the direction of inflation or deflation. This criticism, however, rests partly upon the assumption that disturbances would cause departures from equilibrium of such magnitude that positive corrective measures were required, whereas I should hope that the announced policy, when implemented by annual additions to the stock of money, would result in an autonomous maintenance of a high average level of output and an absence of serious movements in the price index. If this hope were realized it would mean, of course, that neither the possibility of compensatory action nor the drawback of discretionary control of the volume of open-market operations is in reality of much importance. I would lay most stress on the probability that the readily understandable relevance of a stable price level to monetary stability and the incorporation of the possibility of compensatory action within the program would go far to stabilize the expectations of the public. This policy, like those of a stable budget and of a constantly increasing quantity of money, would require annual legislation on the subject of either taxes or expenditures in order to provide for the necessary secular increase in the stock of money.

In an economy with a stable population, a fixed and unchanging quantity of money should receive serious consideration. Even under such circumstances a stable price index would be preferable as a monetary rule, but a fixed quantity of money would then be better as a rule than it would be in an economy in which population was growing. The chief reason for the increased attractiveness of a fixed stock of money would arise from the fact of simplicity of implementation. There would need be no more discretionary action than with an automatic gold standard, and a balanced budget would be consistent with the policy.

VI

The presence of price rigidity and monopoly in the economy would not render a policy of monetary stabilization less desirable. These are problems toward the solution of which monetary action can give only extremely limited aid, but such monetary assistance as can be provided would result from conditions of monetary stability. The strong urge of businessmen and labor unions to strengthen old, and create new, restrictions during depression would be eliminated, although it must be admitted that the penchant for restrictive action would by no means be exorcized. Except for the nearly impossible condition of complete monopolization of the whole labor force of a community, monopoly, either product or labor, is not calculated to create widespread unemployment of great magnitude. The primary effect of both product and labor monopoly is on the distribution of income. Monopolies of both kinds are adverse to the interests of all except the monopolists themselves. They restrict the output of monopolized industries and occupations and thus drive workers into any open segments of the economy that may remain, where they can be employed only as wage rates are reduced. The apologist for labor monopolies is not in reality a defender of the interests of the working class. He is a proponent of the view that the "aristocrats" of labor should be granted an improvement in their lot at the expense of those workers who are already in the lowest income groups.

Monopoly, in so far as it implies price rigidity, nevertheless is of some importance for the problem of unemployment. Particularly is this true of resistance of wage rates and product prices to downward revisions and of monopolistic upward pressure on rates of pay. Such characteristics increase the level of frictional unemployment, and this may be of considerable importance in a changing economy. Furthermore, while monopoly would not itself be a disturbing factor in an economy in which monetary stability prevailed, it would do much to increase the extent of fluctuations of output in an economy in which instability was the rule.

There may be no unique, no simple prescription that will completely prevent private restrictions on the market. Nevertheless, this fact need not be unduly discouraging. If the monopolies, both product and labor, are held to a precarious existence, their evil effects are not likely to be great; and they will not operate to prevent a successful attack by means of monetary policy on the problem of maintaining equilibrium with a high average level of employment.

VII

Not only is there reason to believe that the adoption of a reasonable monetary rule would minimize fluctuations in the level of output; it would equally well avoid chronic unemployment, even though the contentions of the stagnationists were sound. A propensity on the part of the community gradually to increase the amount of wealth hoarded in the form of cash actually amounts to a rising demand for money. This demand should be met with new money. For meeting this demand, the new money might initially be placed in the hands of either the hoarders themselves or the nonhoarders. If the hoarders received the new money it is inconceivable that *under conditions of stability* their demand for cash should rise in consequence of their receiving more cash, and consequently we must conclude that these individuals themselves would be impelled to maintain the level of their expenditures, on consumers' and producers' goods combined, at equality with their incomes under conditions of a high level of employment. If the new money went to the nonhoarders, substantially all of it would be spent on consumers' goods, and this spending would operate to redistribute income between the savers and the spenders in favor of the latter. We can have a high level of employment with any propensity to save (and hoard) that is conceivable in a community of rational men, and at the same time any volume of investment (excluding "investment" in cash) from zero to as high a level as the public may decide upon.

VIII

For the minimal effects of failure to provide for monetary stability we need only consult the past. These effects are bad enough, but there is at least a possibility that the recurrence of severe depressions will sooner or later undermine the foundations of a system of private enterprise and eventually convince the public that a competitive economy is unworkable. Conditions are likely to be so bad as frequently to induce action of some kind. The fact that monetary stability has not been provided will be evidence that the importance of this factor is not understood, and consequently resort will be had to nostrums. As has been increasingly true in the recent past, it is reasonable to suppose that each organized group will ask for and obtain some measure of "protection," of "security," for itself, and this will invariably involve, in one form or another, some decrease in the freedom of the market, some curtailment of output in the "protected" industries or occupations. To be sure, these demands for preferred treatment will be camouflaged by the use of such terms as "reasonable," "fair," "just," "stabilizing," or "protection" from "unfair" or "cutthroat" competition. It will surely be seen that the results of these particularistic programs are not good; but the danger is all too great that, instead of the failure's being assessed on the measures that have been taken and on the absence of monetary stability, the contention will be that these measures do not go far enough. I would not suggest, however, that the sole, or even the primary, force pushing the economy in these directions is to be found in depressed business conditions; but a high level of unemployment will surely magnify that tendency. In this manner the shackling of the economy may well continue to the point where it is felt that the prevailing difficulties can be contended with only by the power of an authority to deal with emergencies as they arise, "unfettered" by general rules of law. One need cite, in this connection, only the current demand of the Board of Governors for more, but still discretionary, power.

Monetary policy is no panacea for the ills of society; but it can be of powerful, even though indirect, aid in dealing with them.

INDEX

A

Act of 1844, 176
Agricultural products, as commodity reserves, 162–164
  prices of, in index to be stabilized, 137, 163*n*.
Automaticity of monetary system, 7, 104–105, 175–177, 219, 221–223

B

Bagehot, Walter, 149
Bailey, Samuel, 132
Bank of England, 107–108
Banks, perverse influence of, on stock of money, 5–7, 34, 36, 41–42, 177, 187
  and gold standard, 7–8
  and note issues, 6, 186
  (*See also* Fractional-reserve banking)
Barton, Glen T., 164*n*.
Beveridge, Sir William, 3
Board of Governors of Federal Reserve System, and discretionary powers, 183–185, 229
  opposition of, to stable price level, 127–132
Bollman, Erick, 10
Budget, balanced, 118–119, 195, 225

C

Carroll, Charles H., 176
Central banking, belief in stabilizing influence of, 8, 175, 178–183
  criticisms of, 182–183
Commercial-loan theory of banking (*see* Real-bills doctrine)
Committee for Economic Development, 172–173
Commodity reserve currency, 159–167, 175
Competitive system, and autonomous responses to disturbances, 1–2, 197
  doubt concerning merits of, 1, 3
  and *laissez faire,* 4
  necessary rules for functioning of, 1–2, 9
  need for monetary stability in, 9
  not inherently unstable, 9, 197
Comptroller of the Currency, 185
Consols, 203
Consumption expenditures and employment, 30, 32–33
Cooper, Martin R., 164*n*.
Criteria for monetary policy, constantly rising price level, 27, 124
  employment, 117
  fixed stock of money, 120, 225
  no one correct guide for, 119
  price level, 117, 159
  production, 117
  speculation, 117
  stabilization, of index of wage rates, 134–135
    of retail price index, 136
    of wholesale price index, 136
  stable price level, 9–11, 27–28, 125–126, 132–133, 196–197, 214–215, 221, 224–225

Criteria for monetary policy, stable rate of increase in stock of money, 123–124, 157–159, 191–196, 212–214, 221, 223–224
Currency school, 176

D

Debt, governmental, extinction of, in expanding stock of money, 191–196
Deficit, federal, as means of increasing stock of money, 195–196, 205, 212–215, 221
Demand, aggregate, 13, 15, 17–18, 23, 69, 197, 202–203, 207
  for funds, elasticity of, 198–199, 201
  for individual products, changes in, and frictional unemployment, 17–18
Depressions, and adverse expectations, 37, 39–41
  changes in stock of money and, 36–39
Diminishing returns and wage rates, 16–17
Director, Aaron, 159*n.*
Discretionary management of currency, 8, 116–118, 131–132, 175, 183, 229
Disposal of income, various possibilities for, 30

E

Equilibrium, general, of neoclassical theory vs. monetary, 1–2, 69
  international, conflict between requirements for, and internal stability, 90
    and easier adjustments under national standard, 88–90
    and fractional-reserve banking, 87–88, 91–92
    income effect on, nonessential character of, 86–87
Equilibrium, international, and increased demand for imported product and required adjustments, under gold standard, 72–75
    under national standard, 75–84
  indemnity and required adjustments in, 84–86
  innovation and required adjustments in, 84
  required changes in real factors of, unchanged regardless of monetary system, 88
Exchange rates, flexible, fluctuations in, and long-term foreign investments, 95
  and foreign investment in equities, 98–99
  and foreign short-term lending, 100–104
  and foreign trade, 92–95
  and forward market for exchange, 93
  limitation on extent of changes in, 97–98
  permanent changes in, due to inflation, and long-term foreign investment, 95–96
    due to causes other than inflation, and long-term foreign investment, 96–98
  speculation and extent of movement of, 94–95
  and stabilization of price level, of domestic goods, 145, 151, 154
    of international goods, 150, 155
Expectations, and depressions, 37, 39–41
  and monetary stability, 9, 13–14, 40–41, 113, 196–197
Expenditures, variations of federal, as means of implementing monetary policy, 205–212

F

Federal Open Market Committee, 185
Federal Reserve Board (*see* Board of Governors of the Federal Reserve System)
Federal Reserve policy, from 1929 to 1933, 44–48, 179–180
  uncertainty of, 8
Fisher, Irving, 10, 63, 126
Fractional-reserve banking, influence of, on velocity, 121–122
  and *laissez faire,* 4
  and monetary policy, 4–5, 177
  and private lending, 4–5
  and specie flows, 91–92
  and stable budget proposal, 168, 223
  (*See also* Banks)
Friedman, Milton, 159*n.*, 167–172, 175, 215–219

G

Gold standard, international, automaticity of, 7, 104, 175–177, 221–223
    and balanced budget, 176
    and fractional-reserve banking, 41–42
    historically a nondescript system, 109–110, 176–177
    losses under, in foreign lending, 99
    and national monetary management, 106–110
    and short-term foreign lending, 100–104
    and stability, 7–8
    and stabilization, of combined index, 151–152
      of price level, of domestic goods, 144, 156
        of international goods, 146–149, 155
  national, faults of, in present system in United States, 113–114
Gold standard, one-country-managed, 108–110, 144–145, 149–150, 152
Gouge, William M., 176
Graham, Benjamin, 159, 164
Graham, Frank D., 159, 164

H

Hansen, Alvin H., 204, 207–208
Hard money, 176
Hayek, F. A., 159*n.*
Hobson, J. A., 67
Homogeneity of labor, lack of, and unemployment, 16
Hume, David, 124

I

Immobility of labor and unemployment, 16
Income, distribution of, and monopoly, 26, 226
  and increase in stock of money in mature economy, 49
Independent Treasury, 176
Interconvertibility of notes and deposits, absence of, 6, 187–188
Interest rate, and investment, 201–202
  and open-market operations, 198–202
  during panic, 35–36
  and propensity to hoard, 33–36
International equilibrium (*see* Equilibrium)
Investment, and employment, 30, 32–33
  foreign long-term, under flexible exchange rates, 95–100
  foreign short-term, under flexible exchange rates, 100–103
  losses in, similarity of, on foreign lending under international and national standard, 99–100

J

Jones, Homer, 223*n.*

K

Keynes, J. M., and classical economists, 60–63
  on desirability of increasing propensity to consume, 49
  interest theory, 52
    attempt to verify, statistically, 52–56
    criticisms of, 57–59
  problem of interpretation of *General Theory,* 64–69
  on stable value of money, 11
Kuznets, Simon, 52*n*.

L

Labor monopoly, 25–26
Laissez faire, 4
Lange, Oscar, 44*n*.
Law, John, 9, 126
Legislature as final monetary authority, 183–184

M

Marshall, Alfred, 61–63
Maturity doctrine (*see* Stagnation thesis)
Monetary agency, desirability of single, 105, 188–190
Monetary authorities in United States today, 183–185, 188
Monetary policy, ends to be served by, 143
  and frictional unemployment, 23–24, 27–28
  and opposition to monopoly, 28, 226
  and stagnation, 49
  and unemployment brought on by labor monopolies, 25
  (*See also* Criteria for monetary policy)
Monetary stability, characteristics of needed criterion of, 12, 118
  and expectations, 9, 13–14, 40, 196–197
Monetary stability, and foreign trade, 111
  necessity for, in competitive society, 2–5, 9–14
  single criterion of, needed, 12
  and spontaneous responses to disturbances, 2, 9, 13–14, 197
  (*See also* Criteria for monetary policy)
Monopoly, and distribution of income, 26
  labor, and investment, 25–26
    and rising price level, 125
    and unemployment, 15, 24–26, 226
  and *laissez faire,* 4
  product, and unemployment, 20–21, 26, 226

N

National monetary system, 111–114, 145, 150, 153–158
Near moneys, 35–36, 122–123, 199–200, 203–204
Neutral money, 119, 134–135
Nichols, Russell, 159*n*.
Nondiscretionary management of monetary system, 105, 175–176, 183
  (*See also* Criteria for monetary policy; Monetary stability)

O

100 per cent reserve banking, 176, 186–187
Open market operations, and aggregate demand, 198, 202–203
  and long-term rate of interest, 200–202
  as means of changing stock of money, 191, 197
  and short-term rate of interest, 198–200

P

Peel's Act (*see* Act of 1844)
Political control of stock of money, 105, 175, 177–179, 182–183
Price index to be stabilized, characteristics of, 137–138
  and inclusion of prices, of domestic goods, 143–145, 151–157
  of international goods, 146–157
  (*See also* Criteria for monetary policy)
Propensity to hoard, and rate of interest, 33–36
  and unemployment, 15, 29–70
Purchasing-power parity doctrine, 95–97

R

Real-bills doctrine, 6–7, 177–178, 183
Reserves and limitation of bank lending, 7
Revenues, variations of federal, as means of implementing monetary policy, 210–212
Ricardo, David, 68, 126
Rigidity, of product prices, and unemployment, 16, 21–23, 226
  of wage rates, and unemployment, 16–18, 22–23, 26, 41, 226
Robbins, Lionel, 111*n.*
Robertson, D. H., 56
Rules vs. authorities in monetary policy, 12, 115–116, 175–176
  (*See also* Criteria for monetary policy, Nondiscretionary management of monetary system)

S

Say's law, 30–31
Simons, Henry C., 11–12, 115*n.*, 126
Smith, Adam, 177
Stable-budget proposals, Friedman's, 167–172, 175, 215–219, 221, 223
  of Committee for Economic Development, 172–173
Stable price level, as goal of policy, objections to, 127–132, 138–142
  (*See also* Criteria for monetary policy)
Stagnation, condition of, increase in stock of money as remedy for, 49–51, 125, 227–228
Stagnation thesis, basis of difference of opinion concerning, 43–44
  depression of 1930's as evidence of maturity, 44–48
  statement of, 42–43

T

Technological changes, and elasticity of demand, 20
  and monopoly, 20–21
  and unemployment, 18–24
Thomas, Woodlief, 116*n.*
Thornton, Henry, 60–61, 101, 148, 179
Tooke, Thomas, 101
Trade unions (*see* Monopoly, labor)
Treasury, Secretary of, as monetary authority, 184, 203

U

Unemployment, frictional, 15–24
  and individual enterprises, 3
  and labor monopoly, 15, 24–26
  and state, 3–4
  and variations in propensity to hoard, 15, 29–70
Unions, labor (*see* Monopoly, labor)

V

Velocity, changes in, and unemployment, 15, 31
  effect of fractional-reserve banking on, 121–122
  offsets to changes in, 44, 112, 121, 123, 159
  and policy of increasing stock of money at constant rate, 157

Velocity, and short-term debt, 122–123, 203–205
Viner, Jacob, 56, 116–117

W

Walsh, C. M., 219*n.*
Warburton, Clark, 37*n.*, 141*n.*

Y

Young, Allyn A., 141*n.*
Young, Ralph A., 116*n.*